How to Correct the 50 Most Common

Mistakes at the Plate

The **Louisville Slugger®** 125 *Complete Book of*

HITTING FAULTS AND FIXES

Mark Gola
and John Monteleone

 A Mountain Lion Book

CB
CONTEMPORARY BOOKS

Library of Congress Cataloging-in-Publication Data

Gola, Mark.
    The Louisville Slugger complete book of hitting faults and fixes : how to
    correct the 50 most common mistakes at the plate / Mark Gola
    and John Monteleone.
        p.   cm.
    Includes index.
    ISBN 0-8092-9802-3
        1. Batting (Baseball).   I. Monteleone, John J.   II. Title.
GV869.G65   2001
796.357'26—dc21   00-46791
                                                                 CIP

To my big brother, Ed,

*Although some innocuous dispute always kept us from
completing our ballgames in the backyard growing up, I wouldn't
trade one pitch for anything. Thanks for your unwavering
support and friendship. In return, I suggest that you read
Fault #27—Pulling the Front Shoulder Out Early.
Trust me, it's been driving me nuts for years.*
— M. G.

*To Coerte, for love of words, and mom,
Josephine, for love of competition.*
— J. M.

Cover design by Nick Panos
Cover photographs (left to right) copyright © Jamie Squire/Allsport,
copyright © Vincent Laforet/Allsport, copyright © Jonathan Daniel/Allsport,
copyright © Matthew Stockman/Allsport
Interior design by Margaret Trejo
All interior photos courtesy of Michael Plunkett

Published by Contemporary Books
A division of NTC/Contemporary Publishing Group, Inc.
4255 West Touhy Avenue, Lincolnwood (Chicago), Illinois 60712-1975 U.S.A.
Copyright © 2001 by Mountain Lion, Inc.
Printed in the United States of America
International Standard Book Number: 0-8092-9802-3

Contents

Acknowledgments

This book was conceived, developed, and produced by Mountain Lion, Inc., a book producer specializing in instructional and general reference sports books. A book producer relies on the special skills of many people. The following contributed to producing *The Louisville Slugger® Complete Book of Hitting Faults and Fixes*. To all of them we say, "Thanks."

Rob Taylor, acquiring editor at NTC/Contemporary Books, whose vision and support was instrumental in putting this book on the shelf, and Heidi Bresnahan, senior project editor.

Bill Williams, vice president of advertising and promotion at Hillerich and Bradsby, for his enthusiastic support.

Randy Voorhees, for conceptualizing this book idea, his contributions to the project and countless morning conversations regarding the world's greatest game.

Michael Plunkett, the photographer who took all the high-speed, stop-action, and step-by-step instructional photographs.

Larry Shenk, Gene Dias, and Leigh Tobin in the Philadelphia Phillies public relations office for issuing media credentials that allowed us to interview and photograph hitters and coaches. A special thanks to Leigh Tobin for arranging several of the interviews.

To all of those who helped in production: Margaret Trejo, design and page layout; Suzanne Davidson, copyeditor; Melissa Martin, proofreader; Colleen Orem of Imagi-Net, high resolution scans; Deborah Patton, indexer; Dave Gallagher, former major league baseball player and model; Rich Brooks, Rider University baseball player and model; Jack Tracy, South Alabama baseball player and model.

To all the players and coaches who gave their time to offer some tips and advice to the many aspiring young hitters across the country: Mark McGwire, Scott Rolen, Charles Johnson, Alex Rodriguez, Will Clark, Mike Bordick, John Olerud, Mike Lieberthal, Jay Bell, Travis Lee, J. D. Drew, Doug Glanville, Jesse Orosco, Hal McRae, Dave Gallagher, and Sonny Pittaro.

A special thanks to Stan Davis, Hopewell Valley Central High School baseball coach; Sonny Pittaro, Rider University baseball coach; Rider University team members (1991–1994); Edward F. Gola; Paulette Gola; and Jason Steinert (Fault #41).

Introduction

"If I'm hitting, I can hit anyone. If not, my
12-year-old son can get me out."
— *Willie Stargell*

For a baseball player, there is nothing more frustrating than struggling at the plate. A pitch is thrown right down Broadway—a perfect pitch for you to hit. You see it well, you start your stride and move your hands back. You're cocked and ready to explode on the ball. You anticipate that ultimate high, the feeling of connecting with the ball on the sweet spot of your bat. You swing. But suddenly, you feel an unexpected vibration in your hands. Something went wrong. Instead of standing on second base with a double, you're shaking your head as you jog back to the dugout. You know something is broken, and you need to figure out exactly what so you can fix it. How to begin?

The issue at hand is not the fact that you made an out. Outs are a part of the game and will continue to occur as long as you play the game. Rather, the issue is why you missed *your* pitch. Did you tense up and overswing? Were you thinking of pulling the ball, which caused you to roll your top hand over too soon? Was it a low strike and you dropped your barrel to the ball instead of lowering your entire body to the pitch? You need to identify what you did wrong and adjust.

This book will help you make those adjustments, to become a student of the swing. The information will enable you to dissect your swing, identify mistakes, and then place yourself on the correct path to recovery and success.

Through years of playing experience, coaching experience, and interviewing some of the greatest hitters and coaches in the game, the authors have identified and analyzed a list of the 50 most common hitting faults. You'll see that we've divided these faults among five sections, starting from the ground up. We begin with problems occurring in the stance, move onto preliminary swing movements, and then discuss faults in weight shift and hip rotation. Section IV, the largest, deals directly with the swing—the forward movement to the ball. Finally, we examine mental errors; faults in your hitting approach, judgment of particular hitting zones, plate discipline, and building confidence.

In Sections I through IV, we begin by defining each fault and examining where the mechanical breakdown occurs. This is very important information because it identifies the source of the fault. Next, we describe the corrective action. In a straightforward manner, we explain the execution, so you can apply that knowledge when practicing the drills that are outlined at the end of each entry.

The final section examines poor thinking at the plate. Many players fear being hit by the baseball or fear failure, especially in front of their peers. Other "mental faults" include poor situational hitting and failing to recognize pitch patterns. This book will help you to eliminate faulty and deficient thinking and foster a positive, intelligent approach.

Each fault has two components: the mechanical flaw and the game result. Acknowledging both elements can assist you in pinpointing your deficiencies at the plate. For example, when a hitter rolls his top hand too early (Fault #41), his swing is flawed. The game result, most often, will be ground balls to the left side of the infield (for a right-handed batter). The "rollover ground ball" is caused by the mechanical flaw. By reviewing the game result, you can trace your steps backwards and figure out your mechanical flaw.

Along with each fault we've provided a comment or two from a major league hitter or professional coach. Most of these sidebar quotes deal directly with the fault that is being discussed. Others simply discuss the general topic of hitting and slumps. These bites of information allow you to get inside the minds of those who are considered the best in the business. Remember, major league hitters go through slumps just like you and have experienced them at every level of the game. Some like to keep things basic, while others are swing doctors who are in touch with each facet of the swing. Listen to what they have to say and see if you can apply it to your own game.

Separating Slumps from the Nature of the Game

There *are* times when you must ignore a bad game. Failure is a major part of the game, and every hitter must learn to deal with it. Understand that no one in the history of baseball hit the ball hard every time. Hitting is very difficult and there are a myriad of factors that can affect your results. So don't make a mountain out of a mole hill. Use common sense the way major league hitting instructor Hal McRae does: "I think you have to give the hitter time to work things out. After 10 or 12 at bats, if he's still struggling to hit the ball hard, you may evaluate what's going on. But a good hitter can come out one day and not feel well, not see the ball well, or his timing might be a little off. Two days later, he gets hot. The main concern is the swings, not simply the results."

What McRae means is that there are times to break down your swing mechanically, and other times when changes aren't warranted. You know your swing better than anyone and should instinctively sense when something feels wrong. Good hitters often assess their swings by "feel" and immediately know when something is out of sync.

The authors cannot stress enough the importance of practice. You've got to swing the bat thousands upon thousands of times to develop into a consistent hitter. This includes swings in batting practice, off the batting tee, soft tosses, and various other drills that are mentioned in this book. Repetitious training creates muscle memory and allows you to stay in touch with your swing. That said, always keep in mind that the game is a time for execution. You participate in drills and fine-tune your swing at practice or on your own time. During the game, it's time to let your muscle memory take over. Your attention and focus should only be on identifying the pitch and reacting.

There is one other important point we should mention. Some of the faults discussed in this book are committed by major league hitters, but they don't adversely affect their performance. Barry Bonds, for example, has a hitch in his swing (Fault #17) and Jeff Bagwell employs a stance that is excessively wide (Fault #3). They're able to "break the rules" at times because they possess superior, innate talents. Major league hitters are exceptionally gifted athletes with tremendous strength, hand speed, and hand-to-eye coordination. We tip our caps to them. Each is truly one in a million.

This book is loaded with useful information. Read a bit and take time to think about what you've read. Then, go back and read some more. You'll begin to appreciate your swing more once you understand its elements. But always remember, there is no substitute for swings. To improve at hitting, you've got to swing the bat over and over and over again. This book will make sure your repetitious swings are executed correctly. Follow this advice and you'll soon be standing on third base after smoking a line drive triple to right-center field, saying to yourself, "Man, did that feel good!"

Albert Belle

The Stance

The all-time greatest hitters have many things in common: hand-to-eye coordination, bat control, hand and wrist strength, among others. Conversely, they also possess many unique characteristics. Each hitter has a slight difference in his swing, hitting style, and, of course, his stance.

Hitters are often identified by their batting stances. If the hitter of conversation is Pete Rose, you immediately think of the crouched position from which Charlie Hustle did his work. Bring up Albert Belle's name and you envision his imposing glare from the batter's box, hands held away from his chest, his upper body perched out over home plate as he awaits his prey.

The batting stance is a matter of personal comfort. There are no set guidelines. There is, however, one steadfast rule that every hitter should obey when searching for his batting stance: *Your stance should allow for a simple and smooth transition that will put you in a strong position to hit the baseball.* If you're holding your hands or setting up your feet in a manner that makes it difficult to get into that position, you need to make an adjustment.

The best approach is to start with a basic batting stance and work from there. If you need to make a minor adjustment or add a subtle movement, make the change from a basic position.

A basic or standard batting stance places your feet just outside your shoulders. Line your feet up square to the pitcher with your weight on the balls of your feet. Flex your knees slightly and bend at the waist. Keep your upper body tall, with your shoulders aligned square to the pitcher. Hold your hands about shoulder level, aligned with the inside of your rear shoulder, approximately 4 to 6 inches away from your body.

Getting to the Root of the Problem

The stance is often the root of your hitting mistakes. It's the foundation of your hitting structure. Many faults originate in the stance. Often they go undetected because too much focus is placed on the end result, which is your swing.

For example, suppose you have trouble handling low strikes. When challenged with this pitch location, you frequently swing and miss or hit weak fly balls to the opposite field. The first thought while troubleshooting would be that you're dropping your barrel. This may be true, but the real problem may be occuring earlier. Perhaps you don't have flex in your legs—you're standing rigid at the plate. This would make it difficult for you to use your legs to lower your body, which allows you to get the bat on a level plane with the pitch, so your brain sends a message to your hands to compensate and drop the bat to the ball. This faulty swing is born of a faulty stance.

Textbook vs. Unorthodox

So does a textbook stance guarantee success? Absolutely not. The proof is in the pudding—and that is the swing. A hitter can set up in the most unorthodox stance and pound balls all over the field. Somehow he gets himself into the proper hitting position before he swings the bat. Hall of Famer Stan "The Man" Musial used an unorthodox stance called the "peek-a-boo" stance. He stood in the back of the box, turned his body away from the pitcher, and peered out over his front shoulder. Rod Carew collected over 3,000 career hits. His stance rarely stayed the same. He changed his stance from at bat to at bat, depending on the pitcher and game situation. Andres Galarraga uses an open stance while holding his hands up near his head. And the Big Cat has hit many balls a long, long way.

Another major league hitter who employs an idiosyncratic stance is Houston Astros all-star Jeff Bagwell. He speads his legs far apart and squats as he awaits the pitch. It's a very unusual (and to many uncomfortable) stance that few coaches would teach. But no one would question Bagwell's ability to punish the horsehide.

These players are using unique stances, but milliseconds later they look the same: Stride foot is closed and planted directly back at the pitcher, front leg slightly bent, hands positioned just behind the rear shoulder. The entire body is cocked and ready to explode on the incoming pitch. Your stance, no matter how unique, must allow you to consistently get to this position.

In this section, we will discuss several faults that originate in the batting stance. We'll examine the way you set your feet, how much body movement you have during your set-up, where you hold your hands, and what your eyes are doing. The stance is the first event in a chain reaction that ultimately ends with the swing. Do things right in the stance and you have a much better chance of making solid contact.

We'll also discuss the grip, the size of your bat, and where to stand in the batter's box. These are important factors in hitting success.

Remember, your stance is a matter of personal preference. But it must allow you to transition smoothly into your swing; otherwise, it must be changed.

Fault #1 No Flex in Stance

Hitting—like so many other highly coordinated athletic activities, such as skiing down a snow slope of moguls or shooting a jump shot in basketball—is a highly skilled athletic movement. It demands keen eyesight, quick reflexes, strength, and excellent hand-to-eye coordination. And it requires split-second reaction—you have less than one-half second to recognize a pitch, judge its speed and its location when it enters the hitting zone, and bring the barrel downward, around, and forward to meet it squarely on the sweet spot.

Use the Athletic Position

If you take a stance without flex in your legs—that is, a slight bend in the knees—you'll have difficulty. The correct batting stance begins with an athletic position. You've seen this position many times in other sports: the basketball player guarding his opponent in a man-to-man defense, the linebacker in football waiting for the snap of the ball, or the tennis player anxiously waiting for serve. Each uses the athletic position in one form or another.

What is the athletic position? How do you use it to establish a proper batting stance? Here's a simple way to establish it. Square your feet and spread them slightly more than shoulder-width apart. Bend at the knees and push down on the inside balls of your feet, with your weight evenly distributed. You should feel balanced and ready to move.

The athletic position puts most of your weight on the balls of the feet. You can stabilize and control your upper-body weight, moving it from backward to forward, or rotating it around an axis (your spine). No one can move efficiently in any sport from anything other than this position of balance and flexibility.

Here are some signs that might indicate you need some flex in your legs, or bend at the knees.

- You easily lose balance.
- You have problems sighting the ball. Poor balance causes you to move your head too much—either up or side-to-side—and you cannot focus and track the pitched ball.

> "There are two key elements to the stance. It has to be comfortable, and it has to be workable. To have consistent success, you can't have one and not the other."
>
> *—Hal McRae, major league hitting coach*

Left: Standing rigid can cause a variety of problems. Maintaining balance will be an issue of concern as will incorporating your legs and torso into your swing. *Center:* To establish an athletic position, stand with your feet slightly further than shoulder-width apart. Flex at the knees and balance your weight on the balls of your feet. *Right:* From the athletic position, you can easily move to a basic batting stance. Simply shift greater weight onto your back leg (approximately sixty percent) and hold a bat off the inside of your rear shoulder. Balance your weight on the balls of your feet and turn both eyes to face the pitcher.

- You are late in reacting. When you try to move athletically—such as reacting to a pitched ball—you must move from a non-athletic position to an athletic position, albeit an inferior one. This takes time—in batting, with a ball moving toward you at 80 to 90 mph, you cannot move quickly enough.
- You're late with your swing.
- You have trouble handling low strikes without flexing your legs, it's difficult to lower your body down to the pitch and get the bat on a level plane. You'll be forced to drop the barrel of the bat down to the ball, thus decreasing your chances of solid contact.

The results? Foul tips. Foul balls to the opposite field. Outright swishes. Frequent Ks!

The failure to flex at the knees also causes excessive spinning of the body instead of driving through with the legs, difficulty in keeping the weight loaded on the back side (drifting is often a problem), and difficulty in hitting low strikes.

Checking Your Stance for Flex at the Knees

Here is a simple way to check your stance to see if you have flexing at the knees. Assume your normal stance with the bat cocked and your head looking toward the pitcher. Then look down at your feet one foot at a time. If you can see the knotted laces of your shoes or any part of the white sanitary socks, you don't have the needed flex. If your knee blocks a view of your knotted laces, and you can see only the forward part (toe box and first few laces) of your shoes, then you've assumed a stance with the necessary flex.

Fault #2 Hot Feet

To have "hot feet" at the plate means your feet are moving around as the pitcher delivers the ball. You'll appear to be taking tiny steps in place and look uncomfortable or fidgety in the batter's box. Hot feet makes it difficult to maintain balance and control your lower body. To swing the bat powerfully, you must stabilize your legs.

Too Hot to Handle

Several problems arise when a hitter has hot feet, but first, let's review the absolutes of a proper batting stance. Stand in an athletic position (knees flexed, slight bend at the waist). The feet are positioned just outside the shoulder blades. Stay balanced on the balls of your feet with your weight shifted slightly back onto your rear leg. Feel approximately 60 percent of your weight on the back leg and 40 percent on the front leg.

Getting Something Going

Many hitters, such as Texas Ranger Ivan Rodriguez and Cleveland Indian Manny Ramirez, lift their front leg up and back before they stride. This is a method of loading up on their back side, a coil, before taking the stride to the ball. A pitcher uses a similar movement in his windup.

Other hitters employ different "loading" movements. Sammy Sosa takes a step back with his front foot before he strides, which works as a reminder to keep his weight back. New York Yankee Paul O'Neill taps his front foot in his stance, kicks his front leg back, and then strides. This technique keeps his weight back early in the swing. The point to keep in mind with all of these hitters is that the back foot remains planted. It does not move. This keeps the hitter's lower half quiet and anchors the body.

Moving your feet up and down (as if you're taking baby steps in place) can disrupt timing and balance.

"When I'm struggling, it's often because I have trouble relaxing. I move my feet and jump at the ball because I'm impatient. So one little thing early on in my approach creates a problems with my swing. I try to understand what I may be doing wrong at the simplest level, and if I correct that, everything else falls into place."

— *Charles Johnson*

By moving the feet in your stance, you can easily lose balance. Your weight may fall back onto your heels or slip forward to your toes. This is not a good athletic position from which to start your swing. Second, hot feet can disrupt your timing. By lifting your front and back feet up and down, you risk having your weight in the wrong place at the wrong time. For example, if your back foot is lifting up at the time you'd normally take your stride, you'll be late striding and getting your front foot down.

Another problem is that your feet may inch out away from each other little by little. By the time you take your stride, your feet may be spread too far apart. This can result in overstriding, which diminishes the power supplied from your legs.

Last, hot feet expose the hitter's impatience or discomfort. Dancing around in the batter's box gives the impression the hitter is nervous. Nervousness creates tension; tension is the enemy of a hitter. Calm yourself down and stay poised at the plate. A pitcher bearing down on what appears to be an impatient hitter will serve up a steady diet of off-speed pitches out of the strike zone.

Hopefully a coach or teammate will notice your active feet and alert you to the problem. If not, these faults commonly derive from hot feet.

Notice how Phillies all-star Mike Lieberthal carries more weight on his back leg in his stance. In doing so, his back foot is unable to raise up off the ground.

- Jumping out at pitches; failing to keep your weight back long enough
- Poor sense of timing
- Failing to get the front foot down in time
- Chasing pitches outside the strike zone
- Difficulty catching up to fastballs

Putting Out the Fire

To eliminate hot feet from your stance, try flexing the knees a bit more. The more flex you have in your knees, the more difficult it becomes to move your feet. Chances are, your stance is very erect if your feet are dancing. Imagine the position you would use to guard a basketball player or goaltend in soccer. Imitate that position and use it as a starting point.

In addition, check to make sure you have a greater amount of weight shifted onto your back leg. This will make it nearly impossible to move your back foot. When your weight is equally distributed, it allows both feet the freedom to roam. Shifting more of it back will keep that rear foot grounded.

Finally, relax. If you're nervous or overanxious, you'll perform poorly. Take a deep breath and have fun.

Left: To keep your feet still, stand upright in the batter's box with no movement. *Right:* As the pitcher begins his delivery to the plate, drop your weight straight down (flexing at the knees) and shift it back to the rear leg. This will keep your feet planted firmly on the ground until taking your stride.

DRILL

■ Assume your normal stance in the batter's box during batting practice. As the pitcher goes into his windup and begins to swing his arm upward, sit down quickly to lower your body (approximately 3 inches) just before you stride. The sequence of movements to contact will be relaxed upright stance—sit down—stride—swing. Be sure your upper body remains tall and your body drops only at the knees. This keeps your feet planted and your body in balance. Also, sit down in time to pick up the pitcher's release point. Your eyes should be set in position to track the ball before he's reached his release point.

You can use this action strictly for drill work or incorporate it into your pre-swing movement in games. Many hitters use this in games and feel comfortable doing so. (Boston Red Sox infielder John Valentin does this before every pitch.) Before using this approach in competition, practice it time and time again to ensure your timing is consistent.

Fault #3 Stance Too Broad/ Too Narrow

When a contractor builds a house, the first item of business is to build a strong foundation. Without that strong foundation, the life of the structure and its stability will always be suspect.

The basic makeup of a hitter is not much different. If you're struggling at the plate, your stance (or the foundation of your swing) is a good place to begin your investigation. A batting stance will not make or break your success, but a flawed stance can adversely affect your swing and contribute to poor results.

The width of your stance is important. Many hitters have their own quirky nuances in the batter's box, but their stance-width is nearly universal. Setting your feet slightly farther than shoulder-width apart puts in you in position to take a short, controlled stride as the pitch is released.

Stance Is Too Broad

If your stance-width is too broad, you'll lose power from the lower half of your body. As you widen the stance, you decrease the ability to rotate the hips efficiently and quickly. Try it. From an overly wide stance it is difficult to create explosive hip movement and you're forced to generate most of your power with your upper body. Your swing path will also have too much uppercut. This will lead to a lot of fly balls, top-spin line drives, and swings and misses.

You may look at the success of Jeff Bagwell and question how a wide stance could be considered a fault. As in all aspects of hitting, there are exceptions to the rule and Bagwell is one of them. His stance is unusually wide, but remember three things about Bagwell: (1) He has exceptional upper and lower body strength. He is able to hit balls out of the ballpark even when using only his upper body. (2) He has very powerful legs and strong torso. This allows him to have an extremely wide base, yet maintain balance and rotate quickly. (3) His stride foot kicks backward and then plants in nearly the same place it started. The front foot of a hitter using a shoulder-width stance would land close to the same spot (as Bagwell's) after his stride.

> "I don't like when guys spread out too far in their stance. I think you lose some balance when you do that, and end up hitting with just your upper body."
> — *Sonny Pittaro,*
> *president of the*
> *American Baseball*
> *Coaches Association*

Quick Fix

Ailments of a stance that is too broad include *trouble getting full hip rotations, uppercutting, top-spin line drives, abundance of fly ball outs, limited power.* If you're experiencing these types of problems, reduce the distance between your feet. You may find you can hit for more power, are able to handle

Left: The hitter illustrates a stance that is too broad. *Right:* After striding, it's difficult to rotate the hips forcefully from this position.

pitches both up and down in the strike zone (increase your vertical hitting zone), and hit line drives that will carry instead of drop.

Stance Is Too Narrow

Several adverse effects can stem from a stance that is too narrow. First, you won't be in a good, balanced position. A narrow base offers less stability. Also, standing too tall can create tension in your stance. Coaches may say, "You look like a statue at the plate." Tension is the enemy of any hitter. Keep the feet at least shoulder-width apart and the knees slightly flexed.

A narrow stance can cause problems when striding and swinging. For one, a batter may stride too far. When a stride is too long, it creates head movement. The head (and eyes) will move forward and down, making it difficult to identify the rotation of the ball, its location, and its speed. By moving your head to the ball, a 75-mph fastball quickly becomes an 80-mph fastball.

Also, when taking a big stride, your weight may shift forward prematurely. If your weight shifts onto your front leg, you will be unable to fully rotate your hips and will rely on just your arms to swing the bat. This not only

"A narrow stance can cause you to lose balance. Usually when a hitter starts real narrow, he gets big with his stride. Even though he's able to stay tall, the tendency is to step long."

— *Dave Gallagher, college coach and professional hitting instructor*

Top left: The hitter illustrates a stance that is too narrow. *Top right:* After striding, the hitter doesn't have a wide enough base to generate power from his lower body. *Bottom:* The hitter displays a workable stance-width that will enable him to generate power and quickness.

Open Stance—Open Book

When you set up to the plate with an open stance, pitchers take notice, and some can read you like an open book.

Hitters open their stance for one or more reasons, but the most common is that they have trouble getting their hips fully rotated quickly enough to handle inside fastballs. To compensate, they move their front foot open slightly (away from home plate) to give themselves a bit of a "head start" in turning on the pitch.

So a smart pitcher will throw an open-stance hitter inside fastballs because it's his weakness, right? Wrong. Because the hitter is so concerned with the inside fastball, enough to adjust his stance to combat it, it's obviously the pitch on his mind. If the hitter is thinking "inside," an alert pitcher will throw the ball "outside"—strikes on the outer third of the plate.

Trouble with Outside Strikes

An open-stance hitter is susceptible to these outside strikes because he's put himself in a poor position to handle them. When using an open stance, the hitter must stride closed (toward the plate) in order end up square and achieve full plate coverage. If he simply strides straight from the open stance position, he'll be stepping away and will be unable to reach outside pitches.

Nine times out of ten, when an open-stance hitter strides, he doesn't get back to the square position. He may think he's striding closed, but in reality, he never makes it back to the square position. This makes him susceptible to outside strikes on every pitch.

Now, if the hitter realizes that he's being pitched away, and as a result closes his stance back up, the pitcher has really got him. He can now throw to his original weakness, the inside fastball, to get him out.

So what lesson is to be learned? Adjustments to your batting stance may help eliminate a weakness, but more often than not, they'll create a weakness in a different area. Focus on the real problem, which in this case is not being able to get your hips through quickly enough. Work on improving the strength and quickness in your torso.

Opening your stance may work temporarily—until you face a smart pitcher—but it will not make you a complete hitter.

---

reduces your power but also makes you susceptible to pitches on the inside part of the plate.

Limited Power from the Lower Body

A narrow base after the stride foot is planted limits your lower body to simply spinning on the ball rather than driving through the ball with your legs. Think about drawing a circle with the use of a compass. When the pencil is very close to the point, the compass is very unstable. The only way to draw the circle is to quickly spin around the planted point. If you slightly increase the distance between the pencil and the leg of the compass, it stabilizes. A broader base will help utilize the power of your lower body.

When both legs are firmly planted slightly beyond the width of the shoulders, they allow the hips to turn. The front hip opens a full 90 degrees—belly button facing pitcher—and the front leg braces, allowing the hips and torso to turn and arms to accelerate through the ball.

A base that is too wide gives you stability but limited hip rotation. A very narrow base gives you quick hips but minimal power from your legs. Standing with your feet slightly more than shoulder-width apart presents a happy medium.

Also, being too erect in the launch position will make you susceptible to low strikes. Because your legs are too close together, you will not be able to lower your body to get the bat on a level plane. The only way to hit the ball is to drop the barrel. This decreases your chance of making square contact.

Quick Fix

By-products of a stance that is too narrow are *overstriding, preliminary head movement, spinning on the ball and rolling the wrists, difficulty handling low strikes.* Increase the distance between your feet. You'll improve your balance at the plate, eliminate holes in your swing, and decrease your chances of head movement and premature weight shift.

"It's important at all levels of hitting to stay behind the ball and see it as long as you can. If your weight gets out on your front foot early, you may still hit the ball, but you won't have much power behind your swing. To make good, solid contact, you've got to train yourself to stay back."

— *J. D. Drew*

Braves outfielder Brian Jordan sets up in a very wide stance. The former NFL football player is equipped with very strong legs and a powerful upper body that allow him to widen his base.

DRILL

■ Setting your feet so they're shoulder-width apart is not difficult to do. The tough part is reminding yourself to keep your feet at that distance when you're in the batter's box. Whether you're in the cage or on the field, draw a line in the dirt wherever you place your back foot in the box. (If you're indoors, place a piece of tape on the floor instead.) Position your front foot so that it's just off the outside of your shoulder. Take a short stride (about 6 inches) and place your glove just beyond the point your foot lands. Before each pitch, check to see that both feet are in the proper position. If you step on the glove, either your stance is too wide or your stride is too big.

Fault #4 Too Much Preliminary Movement in Your Stance

All good hitters have some type of preliminary movement in their stance. It helps to keep you loose and relaxed. It's possible, however, to have too much preliminary movement, which can upset timing and put your body in an awkward position when it's time to start your swing.

Why Too Much Is Problematic

> "Your preliminary movement should be as simple as possible, without starting from a standstill. I prefer some hip movement—a little waggle or a little rock, but something below your waist. A little circle motion with your hands is okay, as long as it's a little circle and it stays slow. You don't want any rapid movement with your hands. It has to be rhythmic and slow."
>
> — *Hal McRae, major league hitting coach*

To understand why too much movement can produce negative results, here's an example. Many hitters like to move their hands in a counterclockwise circle while awaiting the pitch. It's a rhythmic movement to keep the body and hands loose. (Hold your hands as if you're in your stance and imitate this motion.) If, as the pitcher delivers the ball, your hands are traveling down to 6 o'clock, they will be in perfect timing and position for separation (when the front foot strides forward and the hands move backward). If, however, they are moving up toward 12 o'clock as the pitch is delivered, you're in trouble. Because your hands are traveling away from the launch position, you'll be forced to compensate your swing to get to the ball in time.

One compensation will be to immediately pull your hands in and push the barrel to the ball. This is called an "inside-out" swing (see page 119). Another adjustment is to rush your hands back, cut short your separation, and gather less force and momentum for your swing.

Controlling Your Movement

Hitters use a variety of methods to incorporate a preliminary movement in their stance. Some sway back and forth with the lower half of the body. Hall

This sequence shows a hitter initiating too much hand movement. His hands are traveling in a clockwise circle that is much too large. This exaggerated movement will disrupt timing.

of Fame slugger Mike Schmidt used to wiggle his hips as the pitcher began his delivery. All of these movements are okay, as long as they are not so drastic or deliberate that it upsets your timing. Similar to the point made earlier (hands moving in a counterclockwise circle), if your body is swaying forward when the pitcher releases the ball, you'll have poor weight distribution.

Too much movement can become a problem when a pitcher has a short delivery, or when the pitcher throws from the stretch. You simply may not have enough time to go through your routine. Keep things short and simple to avoid disturbing your timing.

Last, if your preliminary movement is too fast or active, it can create tension. Rapid movements tend to make the body stiff. Stay relaxed and keep your body quiet.

Finding a Preliminary Movement That Works

Be clear on one thing; you should have some type of movement in your stance. The laws of inertia state that it's easier to execute an explosive, athletic movement while already in motion rather than starting from a stationary position. Here are a few suggestions for preliminary movements that won't get you in trouble.

As the pitcher toes the rubber, a waggle of the bat can help keep the hitter relaxed. Shown here, Mark McGwire patiently awaits his next tasty hors d'oeuvre.

1. Hands in a tiny circle. Moving the hands in a small circle is fine under two conditions: (a) The forward movement of your hands is calm (not rapid) and does not exceed 2 inches. (b) Your hand position is back near your rear shoulder. The closer you are to the launch position, the less risk there is of your hands ending up out of position. Do not hold your hands up near your cheek.

2. Rock back on your rear leg, allowing your front foot to tap the ground. This is a very subtle, rhythmic movement. Your toes should raise only an inch off the ground. You will feel your weight loaded back, but it must remain inside your rear leg.

    (Another alternative would be to only allow your front heel to raise up and down. Keep the toes in contact with the ground, but tap your heel as you slowly rock back.)

3. Point the bat (with two hands) out toward the pitcher. Hold the bat so that your arms are extended out in front of you with the end of the bat pointing toward the sky. As the pitcher begins his windup, pull the bat back and assume your stance.

Try one of these or come up with your own preliminary movement that feels comfortable. Keep in mind, eliminating all movement is not good. But simplifying and controlling your movements is good.

Fault #5 Poor Positioning in the Batter's Box

Batter's Box: A 6-foot by 4-foot rectangular area, marked with white lime or paint, adjacent to home plate where the batter stands as he waits for the pitch to be thrown. There is a batter's box for right-handed hitters and a batter's box for left-handed hitters. Hitters must keep both feet inside the box while waiting for the pitch and while hitting the ball.

From the above description, you can see that there's a lot of area "to do some business" when you've got a bat in your hands and a hankering—as Babe Ruth said—to "give that thing [ball] a ride." However, the simple act of positioning yourself in the 6-by-4 foot rectangle may doom you before you get to swing. That's because your position and plate coverage are inextricably linked.

In fact, the fault of taking a poor position in the batter's box is almost entirely a problem of poor plate coverage. Some hitters can stand closer to the plate and, because they have very quick hip action, get their hands and barrel forward quickly enough to get the barrel of the bat on the ball. Others cannot—they get jammed with inside fastballs and they must move away from the plate to avoid being an easy out.

Still other hitters can take a position relatively far from the plate and yet cover all areas of the strike zone. Their compensation is often a closed stride that shortens their distance from the plate.

All of this begs the question: Is there a single, standard position that a batter should take in the batter's box?

Yes, the position must satisfy certain criteria, of which the most important is complete coverage of the plate. But one starting position of the stance is as good as another as long as plate coverage is accomplished.

Comfort and Coverage

Comfort is one of the most important criteria. For young players just starting out, here is a simple way to begin. Place the forward foot opposite the middle of the plate. Set the rear foot equidistant from the end of the plate, both feet on an imaginary line that is parallel to the edge of the plate. The distance between the feet should feel comfortable and provide what batting guru Charley Lau called a "balanced, workable stance."

Next, take a stride, rotating your hips, and bring the bat forward as if hitting a pitch. Fully extend your arms and then check your plate coverage. If the

> "When I notice a hitter is standing way off the plate, or pulling off the ball, I'll call for pitches on the outside part of the plate. If they're susceptible to outside strikes, I'll expose them until they prove they can handle a pitch in that location."
> — *Charles Johnson*

Left: For a standard position, place the front foot opposite the middle of the plate. *Right:* Scott Rolen extends his bat to the plate to check his positioning in the box.

Left: By standing too far away from home plate, the hitter is unable to reach the outer half of the strike zone. (Make sure you rotate your hips when checking plate coverage.) *Center:* By standing too close to home plate, the barrel of the bat is outside of the strike zone. The hitter will hit most pitches below the fat part of the barrel and become susceptible to inside strikes. *Right:* The hitter has the barrel over the center of home plate for a pitch down the middle. On an outside strike, the hitter would rotate his hips less, thus allowing the barrel to cover the outer half of the plate.

end of the bat covers the outside black edge of the plate, you've positioned yourself correctly.

From there, you can experiment, moving slightly backward and forward. If your stride is slightly closed, that is, you move forward toward the pitcher and slightly toward home plate, then you can move further away from the plate. Your stride will give you the necessary coverage of the strike zone.

Players with shorter, quicker swings—such as Barry Bonds—can afford to stand closer to the plate. But it is not a good idea to crowd the plate, that is, to take a stance that leaves your hands over the inside of the plate or just off the inside of the plate. This sometimes results in a stride that takes you away from the pitcher toward foul territory. This is known as "stepping in the bucket," and it leaves you vulnerable to strikes on the outside part of the plate.

Signs That You Need to Adjust

Here are some key signs that your position in the batter's box might need to be adjusted:

- You cannot reach the outside strikes (*you're standing too far from the plate*).

"When things are going bad, you start to doubt yourself too much. You begin questioning where your hands are, how long is my stride, where am I standing? You think about too much instead of looking for the ball and seeing it. You need to have a positive outlook. Tell yourself, 'I'm gonna get a good pitch, and I'm gonna hit it hard.'"

— *John Olerud*

- You are getting jammed repeatedly on inside pitches *(you're standing too close to the plate).*
- You are repeatedly making contact with breaking pitches as they are exiting the strike zone below the knees or outside *(you're standing too deep or far back in the box and/or too far from plate).*

If you are a good breaking-ball hitter, that is, you have mastered how to keep the hands back and take breaking pitches such as curveballs and sliders to the opposite field, you can stand farther back in the box. This will give you an edge when hitting fastballs—a split-second more time to get the bat around.

Certain hitting situations also dictate where you stand in the box. For example, if you're a right-handed hitter trying to hit the ball to the right side of the diamond (to advance a runner from second base with no outs), you might move away from the plate so almost all pitches are away from you, and inside pitches (which might be struck on the handle of the bat) are inside and off the plate (balls, not strikes). This will help you contact the ball with the hands leading and barrel trailing and angled so that the ball will go to the opposite field. It will also help you avoid getting jammed, and most importantly, move that runner to third.

Fault #6 Incorrect Length or Weight of Bat

Tony Gwynn uses what he calls his "peashooter," a Louisville Slugger wood bat Model C-263 that is 32½ inches, 31 ounces. It is one of the lightest and shortest models made for major league players.

Babe Ruth swung a Louisville Slugger Model R-143 that measured 36 inches and weighed 42 ounces. Ted Williams's model was a Louisville Slugger W-166 measuring 35 inches and weighing 33 ounces. Bats come in all shapes, lengths and weights and no single model is right for everyone. You must experiment and through trial and error find the model that feels most comfortable to you, a bat that you can control and handle. It's as true in baseball as in basketball, "If you ain't got handle, you got nothin'."

Bat Too Heavy or Too Light

If you swing a model that is too heavy you will develop poor swing mechanics. For one, you will sling the bat instead of swinging it. This is because the weight of the barrel is too much for your hands, forearms, and wrists to control when bringing the bat forward to square the barrel at contact. A bat that is too heavy will not only cause poor mechanics but will also diminish your speed in getting to the ball from the launch position and make it impossible to keep the bat on the correct plane for meeting the pitch.

The hitting results—or lack thereof—will be too many balls hit to the opposite field, too many balls fouled away, and too many missed pitches because you are unable to get the bat quickly on plane and forward.

According to scientists who have studied what makes up optimum conditions for hitting a baseball, the only time you'd consider using an extremely heavy bat is when hitting in slow-pitch softball. This is because the ball is so slow in relationship to everything else that you have enough time to apply a large energy input. That is, you can stand back, wait for the ball, coil, and build up a lot of energy to put into the heavier bat. You probably can obtain the same velocity that you could with a lighter bat in baseball. But in baseball, this doesn't work because you don't have time—pitches are not only curving but coming much faster (you have only four-tenths of a second to recognize the pitch and deliver the bat head to the ball).

Ironically, a bat that is too light can also diminish your performance at the plate and your potential to hit with power. Two of the most important factors that determine how far a ball travels are the speed of the bat and the mass of the bat. If you can swing a 35-ounce bat nearly as fast as you can swing a 31-ounce bat, you will hit the ball farther. The key is to learn the weight at which your bat speed keeps up with the requirement of meeting the ball over or out in front of the plate. For most major league players, the range is between 31 and 35 ounces. Find the number of ounces you can handle without losing bat speed and you've got the optimum condition for power hitting.

> "Let's face it, the size of your bat is going to determine what type of swing you have. If it is too big for you, you're not going to have a controlled, fluent swing."
>
> — *Tony Gwynn*

Bat Too Long or Too Short

It's always best to have a bat whose length fits you best, but if you have to hit with one that is longer than you prefer it is not as much of a problem as with one that is too short. It's likely that if your bat is too long, it's also too heavy. You can compensate by choking up—that is, moving your hands 1 or 2 inches up from the knob. This will give you better control of the bat and effectively shorten the bat.

A bat that is too short will make it difficult to cover the entire strike zone. If you're using a bat that is too short, you'll have to crowd the plate, thus making yourself vulnerable to fastballs on the inside part of the plate. A bat that is short is also more likely to be very light—that is, have less mass. This is fine if your style of batting is to punch and slash at the ball, going for singles and doubles.

Left: If you notice that your barrel is dipping or that you're frequently late on pitches, your bat may be too long or too heavy. Try a shorter or lighter model to increase bat speed and control. *Right:* The ability to keep the barrel on a level plane through the hitting zone is key to hitting consistent line drives.

If You're Starting Out

If you're a young player, age 12 or under, you'll need a bat you can lift and swing easily without straining, a bat that weighs between 24 and 28 ounces. Here's a quick and easy way to determine the right size and weight. Grasp the bat with both hands as if you were going to take a swing. Take off the bottom hand and slide the top hand down to the knob. Lift the bat and extend the arm in front of you parallel to the ground. If you can hold the bat easily in this horizontal position for several seconds, you can swing it easily, too. You've got your starting point.

There really is no quick and easy way for more advanced players to determine the right weight and length of the bat except trial-and-error. The most productive way to find out which weight-length combination is best for you is to start by selecting a weight that you can swing with ease. Then experiment with the length, increasing it until you find the length that feels most comfortable and does not diminish the speed of your swing.

A Tip to Hitters: Choke Up on the Bat

Choking up on the bat is a lost art. Whether hitters are unaware of its benefits or they fear it threatens their manhood is unknown. What is known is that choking up on the bat can help a hitter in a number of situations.

With two strikes in the count, it's a good idea to choke up. Moving the hands up an inch or two on the bat shortens its length, reduces its weight, and increases control. A shorter, quicker swing increases the hitter's chance of making solid contact. It also allows him to see the ball longer, creating more time to assess the pitch's break and location.

Increased bat control is beneficial when a hitter is fooled by a pitch. When this happens, he may have to manipulate the barrel of the bat with his hands. It's much easier for the hitter to make adjustments during the swing if the bat is shorter and lighter. This can allow the hitter to foul the pitch off, or even knock the ball into the outfield, which is often referred to as "a good piece of hitting."

Facing a Fireballer

Choking up on the bat is also favorable when facing a hard-throwing pitcher. Basically, a hitter who can't "catch up" to a fastball has two options. He can start his swing sooner, or choke up on the bat. Starting the swing early can work, but if the pitcher throws anything other than a fastball, the hitter's timing will suffer. By choking up, the hitter, again, shortens and quickens his stroke. The less time it takes to swing the bat, the greater the chance of connecting with a pitch thrown at a high velocity.

A hitter will not weaken his swing by choking up. He still executes the same explosive movement to the ball. Barry Bonds has nearly 500 career major league home runs, and his hands are up on the handle for every pitch. Ask anyone to describe his swing, and they'll use words like short, quick, and explosive. If it's a good enough approach for Barry Bonds, it should be good enough for anyone who steps up to the plate.

Fault #7 An Improper Grip

Ever see a quarterback throw downfield to a wide-open receiver, only to have the ball flutter out of his hand as if it were shot in mid-air? When the receiver asks the QB why the ball landed 10 yards short of him despite lack of pressure, the quarterback responds, "I lost my grip."

Much like a quarterback, a hitter's success is reliant upon a proper grip. Before the swing, before the stride, and even before the stance, you grip the bat. An incorrect grip can hinder performance.

There are two common mistakes you can make gripping the bat. The first is too much pressure, and the second is improperly holding the bat in your hands (rather than with your fingers). Either mistake alone will hinder bat speed, reduce power, and restrict bat control.

Grip Pressure

It is commendable to be intense during every game, for every at bat, and every incoming pitch. Sharp focus and physical aggressiveness are instrumental in becoming a good hitter. However, you cannot allow that intensity, or tension, to leak down into your hands when gripping the bat. As the late great hitting instructor Charley Lau once said, "Tension is the enemy." Gripping the bat with too much pressure will slow your bat down and delay the whip of the barrel. Here is an example. Think back to an at-bat where you worked the count to 2-0 or 3-1 and were expecting a fastball over the plate. Fortunately, the pitcher put it right where you wanted it and you took a vicious cut at the pitch. When you looked up, you noticed you'd hit a high fly ball to the opposite field—a can of corn.

How could that happen? You saw the pitch perfectly and it was right in your wheelhouse. Well, chances are you tried to "muscle up" (or overswing) on the pitch. The additional effort applied to your swing allowed tension to become a factor. Instead of staying smooth and quick to the ball, your hands rushed to the ball and the barrel trailed behind. That slight delay caused the barrel to be late instead of firing through the hitting zone.

When gripping the bat, relax your fingers. Do not hold the bat with a "death grip." Imagine you're holding a ripe peach. Too much pressure will break the skin and sticky juices will run all over your hands.

> "The first thing I ask a young hitter is to grip the bat and swing it. Nine times out of ten the problem is right there. Most youngsters think you grip the bat with your hands. You don't! You grip it with your fingers."
>
> — *Stan Musial,*
> *Hall of Fame player*

Eliminating Tension

Hitters often step into the batter's box with a tension-free grip but are strangling the bat by the time the pitcher begins his motion. Many major leaguers, such as Will Clark, allow their fingers to flicker on and off the bat as they await the pitch. This is called "milking" the grip. This keeps the hands active instead of locked in place on the bat handle.

The bottom line is to stay relaxed and loose. Taking a deep breath or visualizing a calming atmosphere may do the trick. Do not worry about the bat slipping out of your hands with a loose grip. Your hands will naturally firm their grip as you snap your wrists. But to fire that barrel with fluidity and quickness, the hands must start free of tension.

Fingers, Not the Palms

The first time you picked up a bat, you were probably a toddler. It was impossible to grip the bat in your fingers because they were too small and weak to hold the bat. To compensate, you lay the handle in your palms. Unfortunately, this is the start of a habit that plagues hitters for many years to come.

Allowing your fingers to slowly flicker off the handle can eliminate tension in your grip.

Holding the bat in your palms greatly restricts your capabilities as a hitter. It reduces bat speed and power and diminishes your ability to control the bat. Strength and control lie in the fingers of your hands. Burying the handle in your palms restricts movement.

Grab a bat and place the handle in the middle of your palms. Lightly flick the bat back and forth in front of you, as if you were snapping your wrists out over home plate. Now place the handle where the bottom of your fingers and top of your palms meet. Repeating the same exercise, you'll feel increased strength and control when flicking the bat. The hands are less inhibited with the bat held in the fingers.

There are several symptoms of an improper grip. Listed below are the most common.

- Hitting too many balls to the pull side
- Hitting top-spin line drives (line drives that dive downward instead of carrying)
- Pulling inside strikes foul
- Cutting your swing short
- Producing poor bat speed
- Releasing your top hand off the bat

"I try to work my way out of slumps. I hit in the cage, hit off the tee, hit soft toss, take extra batting practice—whatever it takes. I just keep pounding away until I feel good and confident when I step in the box."

— *Mike Bordick*

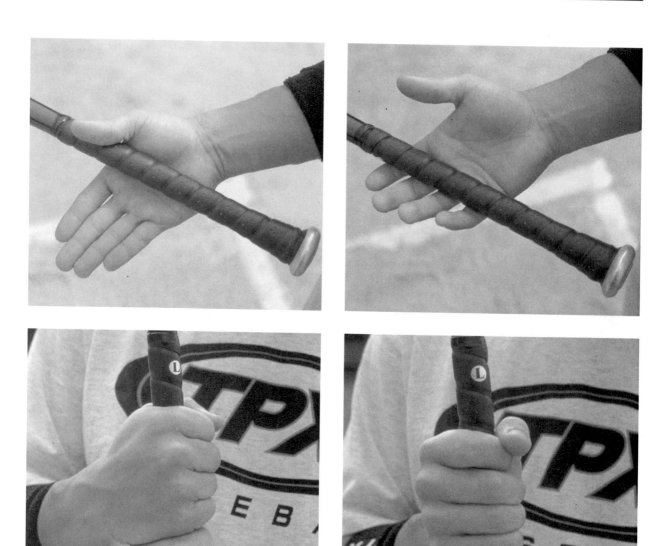

Top left: Never place the bat in your palms. *Top right:* Lay the bat across the line created by the bottom of your fingers. *Bottom left:* A common mistake made by young hitters is lining up the third sets of knuckles. This buries the bat in your palms and restricts bat speed and control. *Bottom right:* The second set of knuckles of your top hand should rest slightly past (or below) the second set of knuckles of your bottom hand.

Grip It and Rip It

To grip the bat properly, lay the handle along the bottom of your fingers (top hand). Roll your fingers over the handle and then close your hand. Repeat the same process with your bottom hand. Apply light pressure with the pads of your fingers. The middle of your palm should not be pressed up against the handle.

To check the alignment of your grip, place the bat on your hitting shoulder and look at your knuckles. Your fingers have three knuckles in them—one just before your fingernails, one in the middle of your fingers, and one opposite your palm. When gripping the bat, the middle knuckles of your top hand should be between the second and third set of knuckles of your bottom hand. What you want to avoid is having your top-hand, middle knuckles aligned with the third set of knuckles in the bottom hand. If you see this, it means the bat is slipping into your palm, which will restrict movement.

DRILL

■ Lay the bat on the ground between your legs with the handle closest to you (at 6 o'clock). Bend over, pick up the bat, and lift it directly over your hitting shoulder. Check the alignment of your knuckles and grip pressure. Repeat this exercise ten times or until you can instantly achieve the proper grip.

Fault #8 Wrapping Your Hands

Any additional movement with the hands can be costly to the swing. With the limited amount of time you have to see the pitch and swing the bat, you've got to be very quick getting the head of the bat into the hitting zone. Wrapping or cocking your hands in the stance can be the reason for the barrel being a split-second late to the ball.

Take your grip on a bat and hold it so it stands perfectly straight. The knob points to the ground and the end of the bat points to the sky. Take your top hand and tilt it about 2 inches forward. This will move the top of the bat about 4 or 5 inches forward. The knob now points to the catcher's feet and the end of the bat to a spot in the sky above the pitcher. When you move your hands back to the loading position, your hands will naturally tilt the bat even further forward. This is called wrapping or cocking your hands. When you wrap your hands, you have to then unwrap them, creating a delay to the start of your forward swing.

Unhinge and Loop

When you wrap the bat, your hands must unhinge before starting your swing. To do so, you must lay your hands and barrel back in a looping motion. At the time you're doing this, you should already be pulling your hands down and forward to the ball. Because the hands are already late, they'll continue this looping motion, drop the barrel below a level plane, and pull the bat to the ball. This is not the path of an efficient swing.

Try this out to get a feel for what's being discussed. Wrap your hands in your stance. Push your hands back to the launch position, moving them back just outside your rear shoulder. Now, in attempting to swing the bat from this position, what is the first thing your hands do? They unhinge and lay the barrel back. This movement has just put you behind schedule in getting to the point of contact.

This fault is easily detectable with the help of a teammate or coach. Simply request they watch the angle of your bat as you prepare to hit. It's important, however, to watch the angle from the time you take your stance right up until the pitch is delivered. There is a chance you may start with your hands in the proper position and then cock forward as the pitcher delivers the ball.

Your game results will be identical to any fault that causes you to be late to the hitting zone. You'll hit a lot of opposite field fly balls, foul off pitches you normally would punish, and swing through pitches—late! The answer is not to swing harder or earlier. You must eliminate that cocking action.

Some may argue the success of major league all-star Gary Sheffield. Sheffield cocks his hands forward as he awaits the pitch and is an extremely dangerous hitter. As mentioned in the introduction, however, Sheffield is an example of major leaguer whose exceptional talents allow him to get away with certain quirks in his pre-swing. His hands are lightning fast, which allows him additonal time to get his swing started.

> "If your timing is off just a little bit in this game, you're going to run into problems. Any additional movements in the pre-swing will make you late. As a result, you'll rush your hands forward to the ball instead of firing the barrel to the ball. It's a timing problem that can be frustrating."
> — *Doug Glanville*

What Is the Proper Bat Angle?

Holding the bat vertical can be uncomfortable. You may feel too robotic and tension can creep into your hands and wrists. If this is the case, let your hands tilt forward (toward your ear) a bit, an inch at the most. This will help your hands to relax. This is a powerful position from which to start your swing, but it will not disrupt your timing or quickness. Just make sure you don't cock the hands too far forward.

Laying the Bat Back

Laying the bat back so it points to the umpire also diminishes your hitting prowess. Many think this puts you in a position to move straight to the ball,

Top left: Cocking the hands and then wrapping the bat behind your head *(top right)* creates too much distance to the ball. *Bottom left:* Laying the bat back puts the hands in a weak position. *Bottom right:* Starting from this position will elongate the swing and manufacture a "slinging" instead of "firing" action.

but the reality is, it reduces your hand action. This leads to a slower bat and longer swing.

When you lay the bat back, your lead arm stretches back, while your rear arm collapses underneath the bat. When you separate, the lead arm bars out (see page 65) and controls the bat throughout the swing. Because the top hand sits underneath the bat from the start, it's never able to take over and fire the barrel at the ball. Instead, the lead arm pulls the bat to the ball and then slings the barrel. This is a futile swing and will produce poor results.

DRILL

■ Take your grip and lay the bat flat on your rear shoulder. Slowly raise the bat up, hinging your wrists away from your body. As the bat nears the vertical position, stop and find an angle that feels comfortable. Repeat this routine each time you swing the bat.

Fault #9 Seeing the Pitch with One Eye

Poor vision skills can limit your ability to hit, and one of the most important vision skills is the ability to track the ball. Eye tracking entails conditioning the eyes to remain focused on an object in its movement toward you. A receiver catching a football, a hockey goalie stopping a puck, and a batter hitting a baseball all require eye tracking.

Two Eyes Are Better Than One

It is difficult if not impossible to track a pitch if only one eye is tracking the ball. This condition is further exacerbated if the one eye with which you're

Left: Batters often peer out at the pitcher with just one eye. *Right:* Turn your head to see the pitcher with two eyes. It may double your chances of hitting the ball hard.

tracking the ball is your non-dominant eye. The dominant eye is the eye that focuses and sends the signal along the optic nerve to the brain.

Most people are what optometrists call same-side dominant, meaning if you're right-handed, your right eye is probably your dominant eye. Unfortunately, this means that in baseball a same-side dominant hitter would have the weaker eye closer to the pitch. Those who are opposite-side dominant have their stronger eye closer, affording them the advantage of being able to recognize the pitch a split-second sooner.

To determine your dominant eye, roll up a piece of 8½- by 11-inch paper like a telescope. Looking through the makeshift telescope, focus on an object 6 to 8 feet away (such as a doorknob). As you're looking through the telescope, close your left eye. If you can still see the doorknob through the telescope, your left eye is your dominant eye. If not, try closing your right eye. You will see the doorknob through the telescope, meaning your right eye is your dominant eye.

How do you know if you're having problems tracking the ball? Here are a few signs.

1. You're swinging through pitches, making no contact whatsoever.
2. You are failing to pick up the differing spins, rotations, and arcs of pitches. This prevents you from recognizing what pitch—fastball, curveball, change-up—is approaching you. This disrupts your timing. The results are disastrous: you swing late on one pitch, early on another.
3. You are "feeling for the pitches," that is, you are not attacking purposefully from the launch position. Your swing is halting and lacks fluidity. Poor sighting of the ball makes you hesitate.

Adjust Your Head Position

How can you solve this problem? For starters, try repositioning your head. You may not have your head turned enough toward the pitcher so that both eyes can see the ball. In this case, the best solution is simply to rotate your head until it fully faces the pitcher.

A good way to check proper positioning is to take your stance in front of a mirror. Turn your head until your opposite side ear is visible. Now, you're in position to allow both eyes to track and focus on the pitch. The dominant eye, regardless of where it's located (right or left), will take over and get the message to the brain properly. Before leaving the mirror, check also to make sure that your head is not turned at an angle that is too extreme (15 to 45 degrees). Your head should be nearly vertical, both eyes level or leaning only at a slight angle (5 to 10 degrees) toward the plate. This position allows you to track the ball with two eyes while keeping your vision over home plate.

"I can't stress enough about seeing the ball and hitting it. That's something people tend to forget to talk about. If you don't see it, you're not going to hit it. If you're thinking about something else other than seeing the baseball, you've got no chance. When I'm on-deck, I'm just thinking about seeing the baseball, and then seeing myself hit the ball hard."

— *Mark McGwire*

Mark McGwire

Pre-Swing Movements

Imagine trying to hit from a complete standstill—no movement of the hands, no coiling action, no stride, no separation—just swinging the bat from an inert position. Your hits would come sparingly and be devoid of power. You must have some preliminary movement to generate fluidity and power.

What is a pre-swing movement? A slight inward knee turn (which can act as your coil) is a pre-swing movement. Moving your hands back before swinging the bat, tapping your front foot back, and striding are all examples of preliminary movements. Some are simpler than others.

Major league hitters use all types of idiosyncratic movements to help get themselves started. Many use them to stay loose, while others use them for a specific purpose. Hall of Famer Joe Morgan flapped his rear elbow in order to stop himself from cocking his bat and then dipping his back shoulder. Nomar Garciaparra constantly grips and regrips the bat to keep tension out of his hands. Paul O'Neill lifts his lead leg before he strides to "keep my weight back first, and then it gets everything into my swing. The longer you carry your weight on your back leg, the longer you can dictate when you want to go to the ball."

As you'll read in this section, you must get some preliminary movement going back first before moving forward to the ball. This is true of most athletic movements. The hockey player hitting a slap shot, the lacrosse player firing a shot on goal, even a volleyball player striking a kill-shot all have motion going back to create greater force moving forward.

Several swing faults are associated with the preliminary movement stage. Some hitters have too much preliminary movement and are not ready to hit once the ball is released. This causes them to be late on the pitch or forces them to rush their swing, which compromises its quality. Other hitters have no movement at all. They attempt to initiate their swing while standing rigid.

At times, hitters employ movements that put them in a poor position to swing the bat. For example, during separation, a hitter may move his hands back past his rear shoulder and then upward before swinging the bat. This is called a "double-cock," and it's a problem discussed in detail in this section.

The one pre-swing movement that causes the most problems is the stride. Hitters stride in the wrong direction, move the incorrect length, carry too much weight with their stride, fail to get the stride foot down in time, and fail to stiffen their stride leg after it's planted.

The stride is a crucial component of successful hitting. Let's quickly review what *should* happen when you take your stride. The lead leg should take a soft, quiet step directly back at the pitcher. The foot should remain closed, that is, parallel to the pitching rubber. The distance of your stride should be approximately 4 to 8 inches.

As mentioned earlier, the stride should be soft, so your leg will be a little bent when it lands. After your foot plants, however, the leg should stiffen, allowing it to accept and control your weight transfer. If the stride leg remains bent, it will be unable to control your weight transfer, and your position will be unbalanced. This leads to "front-foot hitting," which is covered in "Bent front leg" (see page 56).

To reiterate, you *must* have some preliminary movement leading into your swing. Keep it as simple as possible. The more activity you have in your pre-swing, the greater chance you'll disrupt your timing and find yourself in a poor position to start your forward swing.

Fault #10 No Coil in Torso

Like a good golf swing, a proper baseball swing employs coiling (and uncoiling) of the torso. Failure to create this coil results in a swing that inhibits hip and shoulder rotation, and ultimately hinders hand and bat speed. This results in weakly struck hits and balls hit to the opposite field.

Coil the Inside, Fire the Outside

Think of your spine as the center of two concentric circles—when viewed from overhead, the hips scribe the inside circle and the hands trace the outside. When you swing correctly, you coil (and uncoil) the inside and fire the outside, much like a golfer's swing.

Unlike the golf swing, however, the coiling and uncoiling action of a baseball swing is less pronounced, that is, the degrees of turning away from the pitcher (in golf, the target line) are fewer. The reason is the amount time needed to complete a swing. When a baseball is speeding toward you at up to

Left: Without creating some movement going back, you'll fail to generate maximum force heading into the pitch. *Right:* A coiling action can be as simple as a slight inward knee turn. As the pitcher begins to move forward at you, you should turn away from him.

95 mph, you do not have the time to make big turns of the hips and shoulders away and back toward the pitcher. You have, in fact, about four-tenths (.4) of a second.

In golf, where the ball is stationary and you have as much time as you care to take, the optimum coils for maximum power are 90 degrees with the shoulders and approximately 45 degrees with the hips. In baseball the optimum coils are more modest. Ideally, the hitter who strives to hit more for high average than power alone turns approximately 5 to 8 degrees with the hips and 12 to 15 degrees with the shoulders. Power hitters turn their shoulders further away from the pitch, but this position is not for everyone.

The Secret to Griffey Jr.

Among major league hitters there are notable exceptions to these approximate coil percentages. Ken Griffey Jr., for one, is able to rotate his shoulders well beyond 15 degrees—in some swings, as much as 60 degrees or more—

Ken Griffey Jr. employs a tremendous shoulder turn
(inward), augmenting the amount of force he carries to
the ball.

and still get his hands and bat head into the hitting area before the ball
reaches home plate. Griffey is an exceptionally gifted athlete who uses this
increased torque—and hence, energy—to propel the ball a long way. However, until you've mastered meeting the ball consistently forward in the hitting zone, don't try to increase your shoulder coil.

Any further coiling of the shoulders puts the hands too far behind the back
shoulder and creates too great a distance for them to travel to meet the ball.
On pitches hit straightaway the hands and bat head do not square up; that
is, the head of the bat does not reach an angle perpendicular to a line that
leads directly to the pitcher, until the hands and bat head reach a point
even with the heel of the stride foot. Thus, if you coil too much, the bat
head will always trail the hands and your hits will go to right field (if you're
right-handed).

With a coil that is too severe, you will never be able to pull the ball. You
can see how amazing Ken Griffey's swing really is—he pulls pitches regularly
as well as hits with power to the other fields (center and left).

In addition to trying the drill that follows, here is a quick review of how to
position yourself to make a correct coil.

1. Close hips slightly (5 to 8 degrees).
2. As you stride, move hands back 2 to 3 inches.

This position creates the tension in the torso that is necessary for the rapid uncoiling upon planting the heel of the stride foot. Think of your torso as a twisted rubber band—when you let it go, it untwists. When your shoulders untwist, or uncoil, the energy is transmitted to the hands and bat head by way of the arms. This is where you generate bat speed—and power!

DRILL

■ Here is a simple way to build a coil into your stance and swing. Grip and pick up the bat directly in front of your sternum (middle of your torso). Raise it so that the end of the barrel points straight upward. Move your hands up until the top of them reaches a level across from your chin.

Next, slide your hands and bat back to a point directly over your rear foot. At the same time, turn your head toward the pitcher, keeping your eyes looking forward. Let the bat head move away from perpendicular (barrel moves backward and downward) until it rests comfortably yet securely in your hands.

You should feel a stretching along the left side of your waist and across the back. The shoulders are turned away from the pitcher slightly more than the hips. This slight difference of coiling between the hips and the shoulders creates this tension you feel in the back muscles. The coiling is completed when the hands move backward slightly to the launch position (see Glossary). When the heel of the stride foot is planted, the hips fly open when the rear leg drives around the axis of the spine. The shoulders uncoil next, bringing the arms, hands, and barrel of the bat flying through the hitting zone.

> "When I'm experiencing problems at the plate, it's usually not with my swing but with getting something started. I'll have a little difficulty getting my rhythm going so I'll try a leg kick or a leg tap. Just a little something to help get everything going."
>
> — *Travis Lee*

Fault #11 Overstriding

Keep the Stride Short and the Long Hits Will Come

The fault of overstriding—making an overly long step toward the pitcher—has plagued batters since the game began. Baseball legend Branch Rickey, who played, coached, managed, and owned major league teams for more than half of the twentieth century, once summed up the problem:

Left: The hitter is in the stance position; feet slightly outside his shoulders. *Right:* The hitter overstrides. He has lost leverage and will be forced to hit primarily with his upper body.

> "Overstriding is often caused by hitters who have too much movement in their stance and pre-swing. If the hitter is overstriding, try to get him to quiet things down a bit and simplify his preliminary movement."
>
> — *Sonny Pittaro, college coach*

"A man who definitely overstrides can't hit. Overstriding is a brain lesion—it's a timing process of the mind that the man cannot judge clearly, and he steps too far. He's a home run hitter on certain pitches. But when the pitcher starts changing speeds and throwing balls that deflect from a straight line—when those combinations come upon him—he's finished. [Joe] DiMaggio brings his foot up and puts it right down in the same place; [Dick] Sisler strides 6 inches, and I don't know of any great hitters who aren't short striders."

The Host of Problems

Overstriding causes a batter to significantly lower his head and eyes, thus hampering the tracking of the ball's flight. It also causes the batter to lengthen the time duration of his swing. Result? Too many balls are struck back in the strike zone and on the handle of the bat. Overstriding also prevents a batter from uncoiling or rotating fully on the inside pitch. His feet are spread too far away from the axis or center of his body, and thus he cannot rotate as fast as is necessary. It is hard to get the head of the bat out in front, which results in getting jammed.

Proper stride technique calls for a short, quiet step toward the pitcher. The length of the stride can vary from a very short stride, perhaps 2 to 4 inches, to 6 to 8 inches. Anything longer and your eyes will not be able to adjust. Some players prefer to lift the stride leg and foot and then put it back down in nearly the same spot. Try this and if it works, stay with it.

Some hitters are successful by not striding at all. For example, Boston Red Sox Nomar Garciaparra simply lifts his heel when waiting for the pitch and drops its down quickly when he swings. It works for Nomar, but it's not recommended for everyone.

DRILL

■ Take your normal stance and position in the batter's box. Ask a coach or teammate to place a bat on the ground approximately 4 to 6 inches in front of and parallel to your front foot. Take some practice strides so you

Left: Scott Rolen exhibits a short, soft stride that allows him to maintain balance and keep his head still. *Right:* To control the length of your stride, place a bat approximately 4 to 6 inches ahead of your front foot in your stance. Practice taking your stride to feel the correct distance. Next, take batting practice, leaving a bat on the ground.

get a feel for striding the proper distance. Next, have your partner feed you soft toss and take live swings. The bat on the ground should remain in place.

Finally, take swings off batting practice pitching. Keep the bat in position until you've proven you're able to stride the proper distance without fail.

Fault #12 Striding Too Closed/ Too Open

One of the biggest fallacies in hitting is that a hitter strides to where the pitch is thrown. In other words, if the pitch is outside, step toward the plate. If the pitch is inside, step away from the plate. This is absolutely untrue. There is simply not enough time. From the time a pitch is released, a hitter has approximately four-tenths of a second to recognize the pitch, decide whether to swing, and then swing the bat. A hitter strides as (or just before) the pitch is being released.

To become a complete hitter, stride square on every pitch. Striding square means stepping directly toward the pitcher. This enables you to hit inside, middle, and outside strikes. Striding open (away from home plate) or striding closed (toward home plate) leads to several problems.

Striding Closed

A common mistake of young hitters is striding open. To break that habit, they overcompensate by striding closed. This adjustment invites several new problems.

By striding closed, your hips will not be able to fully rotate. Coaches refer to this as the hips being "blocked" or "tied up." Without explosive hip rotation, bat speed and power will suffer. You will also become susceptible to pitches over the inside part of the plate. Striding closed will close off your shoulders as well, trapping your hands behind your rear shoulder. Studious pitchers who observe your stride will feed you a steady diet of hard pitches thrown under your hands.

Poor Adjustments—Casting, Rolling, Inside-Out

On pitches down the middle, hip rotation is significant in getting the barrel out and driving through the ball. If your hips are blocked or tied up, the bat head will be late to the ball. Your brain will send the message to your arms to compensate. Your arms will cast the bat out in front of the plate in an effort

> "Kids should always stride directly toward the pitcher. A lot of young kids either have a little fear of the baseball or are trying to pull everything. Take a short stride back at the pitcher for the best results."
>
> — *Mark McGwire*

Left: The hitter takes a stride in the direction of home plate. This is a closed stride. *Right:* From this position, the hitter will have difficulty handling an inside fastball.

to get the barrel to the ball. This is called swinging with "all arms." The bat will have only the force of your upper body behind it. In addition, casting the bat out (see page 116) instead of firing the barrel in a direct line is a longer, slower path to the ball. This means you have to start your swing sooner, giving you less time to identify the pitch and react to its speed and location.

In most cases, your wrists will roll over prematurely in an effort to put the barrel on the ball. Your result will be a lot of ground balls to the "pull-side" of the infield.

Inside strikes present an even bigger problem when striding closed. Hitters make one of two adjustments to their swing to make contact. Both adjustments manufacture less-than-ideal swings and results. The first is to cast the bat way out in front of the plate and quickly roll or flick the wrists. The hitter will get jammed frequently or chop a lot of ground balls. (If you do hit the ball off the sweet spot of the barrel, it may even be difficult to keep the ball in fair territory.) The second type of swing is an "inside-out" swing (see page 119). In an inside-out swing the hitter pulls his arm in toward his body, leads

Left: Striding open (or stepping in the bucket) takes the hitter's front foot away from home plate. Because his body is moving away from home plate, he's susceptible to outside strikes. *Right:* He'll be forced to reach for the ball, which inevitably causes the barrel to drop. Any movement away from the ball weakens the hitter's position.

with the bottom hand, and pushes the barrel at the ball. Balls are hit to the opposite field with very little power.

To get a feel for how striding closed can tie you up, grab a bat and get into your stance. Take a stride toward home plate, and visualize a pitch traveling to the inside corner. Your legs are tied up, aren't they? The only chance of getting the barrel on the ball is to alter your swing in a negative manner. This hurts performance and consistency.

Striding Open

Striding open (often referred to as stepping in the bucket) is one of the most common mistakes of young hitters. Hitters stride open for one of two reasons: (1) They're afraid of being hit by the ball. A ball is being thrown toward them and instinct tells them to step away from it. (2) They visualize themselves pulling the pitch before it's released.

Assess which category you fall under, confront the issue, and reform your mental approach.

Loss of Hip Torque, Plate Coverage

An open stride opens your hips prematurely. This reduces the power normally generated from the torque of your hips.

On middle and outside strikes, your body is pulling off the ball when you step in the bucket. To make contact, you're forced to let the bat drag behind your hands to keep it in the hitting zone. When the barrel drags behind, it often dips or drops and catches the bottom half of the ball at contact. The result—a lot of lazy fly balls to the opposite field. Striding square allows you to swing through the ball. Striding open forces you to pull off the ball.

Last, stepping away from the plate reduces plate coverage. You may have to literally stretch out to reach pitches on the outside corner. Have you ever felt you were sticking your rear end out and then stretching for the ball with your arms just to make contact? This happens because your body is moving away from the plate and then tries to quickly adjust once you recognize the pitch is outside. By stepping in the bucket, your swing path will cover from the middle of the plate to a ball off the plate inside. Outside strikes will kill you.

To become a complete hitter, train yourself to stride square to the pitcher. You'll hit inside and outside strikes and do so with your body in balance

"When you do not stride square to the pitcher, you're giving something up at the plate. If you stride open, you're giving up the pitch away and if you stride closed, you're giving up the pitch in. This can be strategic at times, though. When I faced Nolan Ryan with no runners on base, I would give up the pitch away and look for the pitch in. That was basically because if he came too far in, I could get the hell out of the way before he broke any bones and put me on the DL."

— Hal McRae, major league hitting coach

Using this drill, you'll step on a bat when you stride anywhere but square.

and under control. Even if you're comfortable starting from an open or closed stance, stride square to the pitcher. It will undoubtedly provide the best results.

DRILL

■ Set yourself up in a square stance. Place two bats on the ground perpendicular to your lead foot. One bat should extend out from just off your toe toward the pitcher's mound, and the other from just off your heel to the pitcher's mound. Take your stride and make sure your foot remains between the two bats.

If you have an open or closed stance, keep the bats in the same position. Remember, your stride should always end up in the square position.

Fault #13 Drifting

Analyzing your results is the best way to detect a swing fault. But what happens when your poor results are inconsistent? Imagine hitting a rollover ground ball to the shortstop, followed by a lazy fly ball to right field. Next, you strike out on three straight pitches in the dirt, and finally, get jammed on an inside fastball, hitting a harmless humpback liner to the second baseman. Have you simply lost it as a hitter? Probably not. The problem may not even lie with your swing. You may be drifting.

Drifting is a fault that is more problematic for rotational hitters (see page 92). It occurs shortly after you've taken the stride. Instead of moving slightly forward and then stopping, the body continues to "drift" forward. Your weight gets too far forward, making it difficult to fire your hips. Your hands move forward, making it difficult to fire the head of the bat. And your head continues to move toward the ball, making it difficult to track the pitch.

What Should Happen

To gain a better understanding of why drifting causes problems, let's review what is supposed to happen once you take your stride.

Your stride should be a short, soft step toward the pitcher. If you're primarily a rotational hitter, your weight has not shifted forward. As the hips begin to rotate and the hands move to the ball, your upper body experiences minimal linear movement. The head moves slightly forward and down at this point. As the hips and hands continue, your front leg becomes rigid and stops any further forward movement. This allows your hips to rotate and to generate powerful torque (which produces maximum bat speed), and your eyes to lock onto the pitch.

What Should Not Happen

If you drift and the upper body continues to move forward, balance, power, and bat speed are lost. Your eyes will have trouble tracking the pitch because they are moving. Fastballs will seem faster, and breaking balls will be darting all over the place. You'll have little hope of solid contact, and when you do make contact, your upper body is your sole source of power; that's not enough.

You need the power that is generated by your lower body. Try hitting from your knees and you'll quickly become a believer in how important the legs are to your swing.

How Do I Know I'm Drifting?

Drifting can be a tough habit to detect. If you feel yourself hitting off your front foot a lot, or if you're "feeling" for pitches (see page 148) instead of

Drifting often occurs when a hitter stands too tall and distributes his weight evenly in his stance. Upon striding, his weight carries forward to his front foot. His head and eyes also move forward, making it difficult to track the ball.

attacking them, you may be drifting. Another checkpoint is your body position after taking a pitch. Are you in a balanced, power position, or are you leaning out on your front foot? To assess your body position, try this exercise.

With a pitcher throwing from three-quarters to full distance (60 feet, 6 inches), take normal batting practice swings. A teammate should stand in the on-deck circle and call out "Take!" on random pitches as the pitcher releases the ball. Check your position on these pitches. Your stride foot should be down, hands in the launch position, weight centered and balanced. Your hips may have slightly rotated; this is okay. Make sure your weight (and upper body) are not out over your front leg.

How to Stop Drifting

Once you've determined that drifting is the root of your troubles, the next step is to train your mind and body to keep your weight back. Think about letting the ball get as deep as possible, then exploding on the ball with your hips and hands. Tell yourself, "Stay back and explode. Stay back and explode. Stay back and explode." Let the ball get to you.

When the stride foot lands, the weight should remain back on your rear leg, poised to explode on the pitch.

The Toe Tap

Adapted as a variation to the knee lift, hitters are now using a "toe tap." A toe tap is used by the hitter during the pitcher's windup. As the pitcher begins his armswing, the hitter takes his front foot, moves it approximately 4 to 6 inches straight back, taps the ground, and then takes his stride.

Major league ballplayers like Sammy Sosa and Chipper Jones have made this pre-swing movement popular. Judging by the amount of success those two hitters have had, it's a technique worth experimenting with in the batting cage.

Sosa began using the toe tap to remind himself to keep his weight back. An aggressive, wild swinger early in his career, Sosa felt he needed to keep his weight back longer. This allowed him to see pitches better and keep his body under control as he attacked the ball. As a result, he's hit for a higher average, and increased his home run production.

The reasoning behind the toe tap is similar in principle to the knee lift. You load your weight back to generate maximum force into your swing. The major difference is that moving the front foot back and tapping the ground is a much more subtle and controlled movement than raising the front leg. It's easier to maintain balance and control of your weight shift.

If you feel too stiff or are swinging from a dead standstill, work this movement into your batting and see how if feels. It sure worked for Sammy. His toes are still tapping.

Sometimes you just need to experience what it feels like to keep your weight back as you stride. To accomplish this, stand on the back of the pitcher's mound facing home plate. Get into your batting stance and stride uphill. Your weight will remain on your back leg. This is what it should feel like on flat ground.

Remember, the stride has to be short and soft. It should never be so deliberate that is causes the top of your body to move over your front leg. Imagine testing the ice on a pond to see if it will hold your weight. Step very lightly without pressing any weight forward. Put too much weight on your front foot and you might fall in some cold water and sink . . . and drag your batting average down with you.

DRILL 1

■ Stand on a pitcher's mound on an incline (so you're facing uphill). Get into your batting stance and practice your stride. Because you're striding uphill, you'll be able to feel the weight remaining on your back leg. This is the same "feel" you should have when striding on flat ground.

"Sometimes I'll drift and jump out on my front side a little bit. If I'm not seeing the ball well, it's not because I'm not looking for it, it's a result of drifting out and having head movement. When that's happening, I've got to tell myself to keep my weight on my back side longer, and keep my head still."

— *J. D. Drew*

Take your stride on an uphill slope (like a pitcher's mound). This is how your weight distribution should feel after the stride.

DRILL 2

■ With a pitcher throwing live in the bullpen (or indoors), grab a helmet and take your stance in the batter's box. Practice picking up the release point, striding, and separating your hands. Focus on keeping your weight back. Do not lunge or drift to the ball. Watch the pitch all the way into the catcher's glove. This will train you to sit back and allow the pitch to come to you.

Fault #14 Failing to Get Your Stride Foot Down in Time

Get Yourself in Synch

The swing is a series of synchronized actions. It is most effective when a batter performs each action in the sequence at the precise time it's needed. When a swing is not fluid or synchronized, it is rendered less powerful or the power that is generated is misdirected—that is, you hit a topped grounder or a sky-high pop-up. This is what the art of pitching is all about—upsetting the swing's rhythm and fluidity. Why should you help the pitcher by getting yourself out of synch?

Remember: When you fail to get your stride foot planted in time you're helping the pitcher. You're upsetting the timing of the swing, you're robbing the swing of its power, and you're putting some weakly hit balls into play.

Isolating the Root of the Fault

There are at least three reasons for this fault. The first is that your stride is too long. If you're moving the stride foot beyond a reasonable length—4 to 8 inches—you're adding time to the swing, time that you cannot afford to build into the four-tenths of a second you've got to react and hit the ball. Your weight cannot shift forward, your hips cannot uncoil until your feet form a base for supporting these actions. With a stride that is too long, you're still getting settled when you should be transferring your weight and uncoiling your hips.

Another reason for failing to get the stride foot planted is the bad practice of keeping the weight on the ball of your stride foot. When used correctly, the stride foot in batting acts like the stride foot in pitching. The initial plant is made with the ball of the foot, but when the weight is shifted and the torso and hips are uncoiled, the entire foot braces and absorbs the weight. If you swing on the balls of your stride foot you will lose balance and diminish your ability to hit with power. The forces of the lower body are

"If you don't get your stride foot down in time, you've got no foundation. You'll have poor balance and very little power or bat speed. This mostly happens when you begin your separation too late. You've got to give yourself enough time to push your hands back and get your foot down."

— *Alex Rodriguez*

Left: At this point in the ball's flight, the stride foot should be planted on the ground. For whatever reason, the hitter started too late and failed to get his stride foot down in time. *Right:* The stride foot is down, hips are rotated, and hands are in position to fire the barrel.

Buyer Beware—The Knee Lift Is Not for All Hitters

Originated by New York Giants first baseman Mel Ott in the 1930s, lifting the knee before the stride has become a popular practice of hitters. Ott raised his entire leg in a straight lift to load his weight back as the pitch was delivered. This, in turn, put him in a powerful position from which to attack the ball.

The knee lift, however, can be detrimental if used incorrectly. It can easily disrupt timing, cause drifting, and induce head movement. Young hitters especially experience difficulties when employing a knee lift. Their legs have not developed enough strength to maintain body control and proper balance. This results in premature weight transfer in addition to the problems listed above.

Shifting Outside the Rear Leg

One problem with the knee lift occurs when you allow your weight to shift outside the rear leg. When this happens, your whole body sways or rocks backward. This places you in an unbalanced position. As your knee lowers to stride forward, you'll fall toward the pitcher in an uncontrolled manner, making it difficult to keep your weight back.

Also, shifting your weight outside the rear leg causes your head to move back. It must then move forward when the stride foot comes down to plant.

A proper knee lift keeps the hitter's weight inside his rear leg. His knee lifts as he loads his weight back, but the back leg doesn't rock back. The same can be said of a pitcher. As he lifts his knee during the windup, his rear leg acts as a stable post that accepts the weight of his body, but doesn't allow that weight to move outside the rear leg. If the pitcher does, he'll drift forward to home plate when he lowers his stride leg and lose control of the strike zone.

In addition, hitters often start their knee lift too late. They fail to get their stride foot down in time, which disrupts timing and plagues their swing.

To generate a powerful swing, it's imperative that you move back before going forward. But this movement, or "coil," can be accomplished in a much more subtle manner. A slight inward turn of the front knee while pushing the hands back to the rear shoulder gives you enough backward movement to get into a powerful position.

Remember, the knee lift may have merit, but it's not for everybody. Don't decide to employ a knee lift just because you've seen major league hitters use it. The stride is the most important movement in the pre-swing. Don't make it more difficult than it has to be. Keep it simple.

not fully transferred through the uncoiling to the torso, shoulders, arms, and hands.

The third cause is that you simply fail to move your weight off the rear foot or back side of the body. This leaves your plant foot with nothing to do, no weight to absorb, no planting to help the hips rotate. The plant foot then spins out. Your rear side rotates without any linear movement of the arms and hands toward the pitch. The right shoulder drops and your "best shot" is a pop-up to the shortstop. This fault devastates hitters because they have no foundation from which to generate a powerful swing. Your hands cannot start forward until the stride foot plants. Because your swing is now behind schedule, it is rushed to merely "catch up" to the ball instead of attacking it.

DRILL

■ Here is a simple drill to get your stride foot down in time. Take your stance, then stride as if you're going to swing. Keeping both your stride foot and rear foot on the ground, shift your weight forward over the stride foot, bat pointed at the pitcher. Next, time the pitcher's motion so that when the pitcher drops his hand down, back, and up to deliver the ball, you drop you bat down, back, and up. Time your move so that your hands are ready to move forward upon release of the ball (they've moved into the position taken when they separate slightly from the rear side of the body). As the ball is released (and you've judged its speed and location), shift your weight onto the stride foot, rotating your hips and starting the hands forward, bat head trailing until you unhinge or snap the wrists. Stay balanced throughout.

Your objective is to ingrain the feeling of your stride foot taking the weight shift early enough to allow the hips to uncoil into the front side. Be careful not to shift the top of your body over the front leg. Check to see that your rear leg is forming an "L" shape and that the front leg is stiffening as you rotate.

If not properly executed, a knee lift can create timing problems.

After you are comfortable with this simplified, strideless swing, add back your stride, making sure that you complete the swing as performed in the drill.

Fault #15 Bent Front Leg

Hitting with a bent front leg causes numerous problems. It allows your weight and balance to move outside your front leg, promotes head movement toward the pitch, and slows down the rotation of your hips. All of this translates into a slower bat, less power from your lower body, and difficulty identifying pitches.

Simple Contact—Not Power

During the pre-Ruthian Dead Ball Era, many players hit with a bent front leg. Their focus was making contact and gaining momentum to run to first base.

Left: When the front leg remains bent throughout the swing, there is no post (or center axis) from which the lower body can forcefully rotate. The result is a weak swing that contacts the ball out in front of home plate. *Right:* After the front foot lands, the front leg must stiffen to accept your weight transfer and allow the hips to fire open.

Hip rotation was insignificant because power hitting was unheard of. And the statistics back it up. In 1909, Ty Cobb led the American League with nine home runs.

Since the emergence of Babe Ruth, hitting the ball long and hard has become the goal of good hitters. Ruth revolutionized the swing by stiffening his front leg, firing his hips into the pitch, and taking a thunderous whack at the ball. His style was copied by his contemporaries and remains the most dangerous and preferred hitting method in the game today.

Stiffen the Front Leg

Though the body should remain loose and relaxed when hitting, the front leg is one area that must become rigid to experience success. After the foot plants, the front leg must stiffen up to control weight transfer and allow the hips to rotate with force.

The fault occurs when you fail to stiffen your front leg. Because it is a "soft" stride toward the pitcher, you may stay too relaxed and allow your front knee to bend. Stand up and feel what happens when your front knee bends forward. Your weight and balance move onto your front foot. Because the leg isn't rigid, there's nothing to stop the momentum. Your weight will continue to move forward as you swing the bat, pulling your head forward with it.

Take that same soft step toward the pitcher, but as the foot plants, stiffen your front leg. This stops any further linear movement (or weight transfer). The hips can now snap through with force. Your head remains still and your body balanced over the point of contact.

It may sound insignificant, but in reality, bending the front leg can drain considerable strength from your swing. Stiffen the front leg and reap Ruthian benefits.

"During the last few years with Toronto, I would often land with a bent front leg and wasn't able to get good hip torque. As a result, I would lose quickness and power. When I was with the New York Mets, Tom Robson (hitting instructor) got my hips more involved with my swing. To do that, I had to stiffen my front leg after my stride foot landed. This allowed me to transfer the energy from lateral to rotational and really get my bat through the zone quicker and with more force."

— *John Olerud*

DRILL

■ Stand up facing a wall with your toes approximately 6 inches from the base of the wall. Place both hands against the wall at shoulder height, shoulder-width apart. Spread your feet slightly further than shoulder width apart. Flex the knees a bit as if you're in your batting stance.

With your eyes facing the wall, draw a dot or place a small piece of tape on the wall opposite the tip of your nose. Now, turn your head to look as if there were an imaginary pitcher. In this position, take your stride and rotate your hips. Concentrate on keeping the front leg stiff after the stride foot is planted.

Doug Glanville fails to stiffen his front leg on this swing. As a result, his weight escapes over his front foot and his barrel drops as he reaches for the pitch.

In the finished position, your hands should still be against the wall, hips facing the pitcher, front leg stiff, back leg in an "L" shape, and body in balance. Turn your head back so it's facing the wall. The dot (or piece of tape) should now extend from your rear eye (right eye if you're right-handed, left eye if you're left-handed). If it's any farther back than your rear eye, your head is moving too far forward and you're not stiffening your front leg in time.

Fault #16 No Separation

Separation is when a batter steps forward toward the pitcher with his front (or stride) foot while moving his hands slightly backward just off the rear shoulder into the launch position. The base of the body's core or trunk is widened slightly when the stride foot plants and the hands and wrists have cocked the bat to the rear. You should feel a slight stretching of the shoulders and upper back muscles when you separate your hands.

Faults in separation fall into two categories: (1) failure to stride properly and (2) failure to move the hands into the correct launch position.

Most Move Back to Go Forward

Almost no one fails to make a move toward a pitched ball. Moving in some way toward the pitched ball is a natural reaction. However, inexperienced batters often will carry the upper body forward with the stride step. This is wrong. This fails to produce a separation from the body's core, which must be ready to uncoil in a split second, or as soon as the stride foot is planted and the decision to swing is made. It also moves a significant portion of a batter's weight prematurely onto and directly over the stride foot.

When the stride foot goes forward—generally from a few inches to no more than 8 inches, depending on the height and stance of the batter—the hands move slightly back. They are more often shoulder high or higher, although some batters start their hands slightly below the rear shoulder. The batter is now poised to drop the heel of the stride foot, shift the weight onto the front leg, and rotate the hips and shoulders and bring the arms and hands through the hitting zone.

Notice the position of the hands in the left and center photos. Even though the stride foot has planted *(center)*, the hands have not moved back. Remember, you must go back before moving forward. In the photo on the right, the hands have moved back to the launch position. They are cocked and ready to explode.

Don't Trap the Hands

The separation of the hands can go wrong when you move them too far and get them "trapped" behind the shoulders. That is, they are so far back that they cannot reach the hitting point in time for the bat to meet the ball.

Some players, such as Ken Griffey Jr., move their hands further behind when they couple the separation with a backward rotation of their entire upper body. However, they keep their hands in the same position relative to the rear shoulder. They do not move them so far behind the shoulder that they would then fail to reach the hitting zone in time. Other hitters, such as Tony Gwynn and Paul O'Neill, prefer turning their shoulders away much less from the pitcher. Their separation of the hands is more to the rear and less back and around like Griffey. Players such as Griffey who add coiling away from the pitcher in the separation phase of hitting have exceptionally strong back and abdominal muscles, which control the coiling and uncoiling. In many ways, Griffey's separation and coiling move is to the baseball swing as Tiger Woods's coiling and uncoiling is to the golf swing. Both add tremendous speed to their hands by turning their shoulders farther than their peers.

No Separation—No Power

Players who have poor separation will find themselves making weak or late contact with pitches. Without separation you will lose strong wrist cocking. Instead of firing the head of the bat into the ball you will be pushing it. The result is no pop and only weakly hit balls.

Without the wrist cocking that separation brings, you will be late in delivering the barrel of the bat. The result will be foul balls to the opposite field. When you bring the body and hands forward with the stride—that is, fail to separate properly—pitches seem faster in your mind's eye than they really are and you reduce the eye-tracking time on off-speed pitches.

DRILL

◼ Stand in front of a mirror in your normal stance. Practice "hiding your hands," that is, moving them until they're out of sight. This should position them slightly to the rear of the back shoulder. Done properly, this will also help in keeping your lead shoulder closed until you start your swing. As you move the hands to the rear take a short, soft stride with your toe closed (your foot should be nearly perpendicular to the imaginary pitcher). Plant your foot as if you're stepping on eggshells, or testing ice on a lake for safety. These separations, the hands from the back and the foot from

> "It's very important to get something moving back before you start your swing forward. In our business, it's called loading and it's just a like a prize fighter loading to throw a punch. By moving back first, you'll generate more power."
>
> — *Will Clark*

the front, put you into the proper launch position (the body's position just prior to attacking the pitch). Do this drill daily ten times without swinging (simulate taking a pitch) and twenty times coupled with a swing.

Fault #17 Hitching Before Swinging

Hitching is a down-and-up movement of the hands and bat prior to moving the hands into what is termed the launch position. During the swing when the hands come to a position that is shoulder-level or slightly above the shoulders and a few inches in front of the body, they have moved into the launch position. From there, the hands separate slightly, that is, move backward on a level plane, or plane that is parallel to the ground, as the front foot moves toward the pitcher and plants, toe slightly closed.

The fault of hitching occurs when the hands, which have moved downward prior to the release of the pitch, fail to move back and up into the launch position in time for the short, backward separation that accompanies the stride.

When the hands drop down from their starting position (as shown in this sequence), it's called a hitch.

Barry Bonds uses a hitch as his triggering mechanism. Because he has exceptional hand speed and strength, he's able to compensate for this swing fault.

"When you find yourself late to balls you normally hit hard, it could be due to a slight movement in your pre-swing—like a hitch. Fouling pitches back is going to happen, but if you foul off four straight fastballs on a full count, something is keeping you from getting the barrel to the ball in time."

— *Scott Rolen*

Completing the Hitch Prior to Release

Although hitching is better avoided in developing your pre-launch movements, it is not always a detriment to successful hitting. Some accomplished major league players have dropped their hands—or hitched—prior to moving the bat into the launch position. Baseball Hall of Famer Rod Carew started his swing with his hands low, as do Barry Bonds and Tony Batista. However, they have been successful because they complete the hitch, that is, get their hands up and into the launch position, well before the pitcher releases the ball. These players have extraordinary control of their bodies and strength in their hands and forearms, which enables them to maneuver the barrel or head of the bat quickly up and back into the launch position.

Perhaps you suspect that you have a hitch and are not certain if it needs fixing. Here are some criteria to help you assess the situation. If any two of these conditions characterize your pattern of batting, you might have developed a hitch that needs correcting.

1. Your swing is not catching up with fastballs, especially pitches waist high and above in the strike zone.

Although he's been a very dangerous hitter throughout his career, Andres Galarraga experiences difficulty handling high strikes. This sequence illustrates why. Starting from an open stance, Galarraga closes up and strides square to the pitcher. As he does so, he drops his hands down to initiate separation. He then raises his hands back up to the launch position. This additional movement (hitch) makes it difficult for him to get the barrel to the ball in time on high, inside strikes. As shown, Galarraga is a split-second late to this pitch. Because the barrel arrives late, he pops the pitch up for an easy out.

Left: The walk-up tee drill is an excellent drill to practice separation. Stand a foot or two behind your normal stance position. *Center:* Step with your right foot (right-handed hitter) toward the tee. *Right:* Stride with your left foot, and swing. Execute this in a continuous motion. This drill works because as you walk up to the tee, your hands will naturally move back to strike the ball.

2. You are frequently contacting balls toward the back of the plate, and rarely in front of the plate.
3. You are getting jammed repeatedly on inside pitches of average speed.
4. You are popping up fastballs or fouling them straight back a lot.

Cure Is Easy and Simple

> "Good hitters never really change their swings. They just make little adjustments along the way."
>
> — *Travis Lee*

Curing a hitch is one of the easier batting corrections you can make. First, understand that a pre-swing or pre-launch movement is beneficial to making a good swing. Slight movements reduce tension, and without tension, you can make a faster, more powerful explosive movement of the barrel of the bat to the ball. But if you suffer from hitching, and cannot get the hands up and back in time before the pitcher's release of the ball, try the following pre-swing movement. It should cure what ails you.

Instead of dropping your hands during your pre-swing movement, move them up and back. For starters, exaggerate the movement. Move the hands up 2 to 3 inches and back 6 to 7 inches. Picture yourself "hiding your hands" from the pitcher. Practice this movement against slow to medium windups and tosses. Then have the pitcher gradually increase the speed of the pitches. To find your optimum position for launch, begin shortening the backward movement of the hands, stopping the backward motion of the hands when the pitcher reaches his release point. You should feel some coiling in the trunk and stretching of the left upper arm and shoulder.

This will not only put you into the correct launch position but will also pull your front shoulder slightly closed, which puts your entire front side in the correct hitting position. Remember, the movement of your hands is up, then back. Do not move your hands so far back that they get "trapped" behind your rear shoulder; that is, the hands have too great a distance to travel to the hitting area when you execute the swing.

DRILL

■ This is called the "walk-up tee drill." Set a ball on a batting tee. Take three or four steps back away from your stance position (as if you were standing deep, deep in the batter's box). Take slow steps up to the tee. Stride and swing in one continuous motion. Your natural instincts will be to push your hands back to your rear shoulder—the power position—before swinging the bat. Repeat this until the hand movement becomes habit.

Note: Be careful not to wrap the barrel too much behind the head on separation. If you do, you will create a path to the ball that is too long.

Fault #18 Barring the Lead Arm

To create maximum power and bat speed, your hands must move back before moving forward. (This holds true with all physical acts of force.) In doing so, both the lead and rear arm remain flexed during this stage of the pre-swing. Extending the lead arm back to where it's locked stiff is called barring your lead arm. This fault delays the start of your forward swing, lengthens your swing, and diminishes bat speed.

Moving your hands back to the launch position is a joint movement by both the lead and rear arms. Don't allow the rear arm (top hand arm) to be dormant while the lead arm (bottom hand arm) extends back. Think of your hands and arms as a single unit, a family. The entire family unit moves back just off your rear shoulder in a relaxed manner. If one arm tries to dominate, the result will be a dysfunctional family.

Left: Notice the lead arm has straightened out upon moving back to the launch position. This is called "barring your arm." This often creates a second fault—rolling the top hand prematurely. *Right:* The top hand dominates the swing and slings the bat through the zone. The hitter tops the ball as a result of a top-hand dominant swing.

Stay Flexed for Power

Maintaining flexion in your arms as they move back is very important. It fathers an explosive swing. Refer to any sport that requires the athlete to strike an object and you'll find that the body part responsible for the attack is flexed throughout the backswing. A soccer player flexes at the knee during his backswing. Could you imagine kicking a soccer ball for distance if your leg were stiff during the backswing? A boxer keeps his arm flexed as he rears back to punch. He does this for two reasons: power and quickness. Both of these characteristics are integral to a productive baseball swing.

Barring your lead arm will delay and lengthen your path to the ball. Here is why. Extending your lead arm will push your hands farther back than they need to go, well beyond the rear shoulder. (To follow along, imitate this motion.) It not only takes longer to move back, but it also builds a greater distance to get back to the ball.

This fault often occurs if you hold your hands too far away from your body in your stance. Your elbows have less flexion from this position, making it easier to bar your lead arm during separation. A great example of this is Baltimore Orioles hitting machine Albert Belle. When Belle is struggling at the plate (which is very rare), it's often because he's barring his lead arm. As you may know, he holds his hands out away from his body in his stance. He sometimes carries his arms too far back, making him late to the ball. Of course, telling him that to his face could be dangerous.

Long and Late

When starting your forward swing from this extended position, you'll do one of two things. You'll immediately flex your lead elbow and move to the correct position, or you'll push your hands out away from your body to initiate your swing. The first option delays your swing, and the second delays and elongates your swing.

Your performance at the plate will suffer, and it may suffer in many ways. You'll constantly be late to the ball. You'll swing through fastballs, foul off fastballs, or hit balls below the barrel (getting jammed).

To compensate for being late, you may try to start your swing earlier. This will lead to chasing pitches outside the strike zone. Other poor results depend on which action you take from the barred position. If you immediately flex your elbow, you may slice a lot of balls to the opposite field and experience difficulty handling low or inside strikes. If your hands move out

"I've made a lot of changes over the years to make it easier to get my hands to the ball. I used to lean back in my stance and have my lead arm almost blocking my vision. I looked like Dracula holding his cape over his face. A coach in Triple-A showed me a basic major league stance. That adjustment simplified things and made my swing shorter and quicker to the ball."

— *Doug Glanville*

Here Will Clark is moving his hands back to the launch position. Notice he maintains some flexion in his lead arm as he's cocked back in the ready position.

Timing the Pitcher

What does it mean to time the pitcher? Does it mean time his fastball, his curveball, his delivery? Coaches often tell hitters to time the pitcher while they're on deck but lack specificity. Here's what you should do.

First, time the pitcher's motion. Get a feel for how long it takes for him to release the ball. This gives you a sense of when to start your stride and move your hands back to the launch position. Some pitchers have very quick deliveries, while others are very slow and deliberate. A pitcher with a "herky-jerky motion" is one who has some type of quirky delay or disruption in his delivery. This type of pitcher will give you fits if you don't take the time to decipher his rhythm.

Next, time his fastball. Pay attention to how long it takes for the ball to get from the pitcher's hand to the catcher's glove. Calculating the time of his motion along with the speed of his fastball will dictate exactly when you'll stride and move to the launch po-

sition. Facing a pitcher who throws at a very high velocity, you'll have to start everything a little sooner. Battling a pitcher who's crafty and lacks velocity, you'll start your pre-swing movements a bit later.

Finally, time his off-speed pitches. When you identify the pitch to be something other than a fastball as it's thrown, you'll have some reference on how long it will take for the ball to travel into the hitting zone. Record this information (mentally) before you get to the plate. It's tough enough to identify pitches as they're released. By timing in mid-flight, you're making life very difficult for yourself. By timing the pitch before you're in the batter's box you've gained a slight edge, maybe the difference between an out and a base hit.

The prettiest swing in baseball will produce nothing but ugly results if the hitter has a poor sense of timing. Spend your time wisely on deck or in the dugout and time the pitcher.

away from your body following separation, poor results may include hitting top-spin line drives, hooking balls that dive toward the pull-side foul line, and topping ground balls to the pull-side of the infield.

Fixing the Problem

Realizing you're barring your lead arm is half the battle. The latter half (curing it) requires learning the correct movement through repetition. With every swing, whether it be from a tee, soft toss, or live pitching, remind yourself to maintain flexion during separation.

Also, pay attention to where your hands start from (in your stance); they may be too far away from your body. Hold the bat approximately 6 inches away from the inside of your rear shoulder. This will increase the bend in your elbow.

Remember, think of your hands and arms as a single family unit when moving the bat back to the launch position. Do not push the bat back with just your lead arm. The family unit will suffer.

DRILL

■ Stand in the batter's box and take pitches. Stride and separate your hands with a coach watching closely. Focus on keeping flexion in your lead arm as you move your bat to the launch position. Continue this for twenty pitches, or until you stop barring your lead arm.

   Next, have a coach or teammate flip you soft toss while you're in the launch position. Take your stride and separate, pick up the ball, and swing from that position. Concentrate on keeping the elbows bent as they move back and being short to the ball in your swing.

   Finally, put it all together off of live pitching. If a coach or teammate notices you're barring your lead arm again, go back to square one and take pitches.

Fault #19 Double-Cock

Every pre-swing movement must have merit or it should be eliminated. The goal is to simplify, not complicate your swing. A double-cock is a pre-swing movement that is without merit, one that every hitter should avoid.

Left: The correct movement. The stride foot is down with the hands loaded back. *Right:* The problem is a second movement that travels upward. This is a double-cock and delays the forward movement of the swing.

After the hands separate, they take the barrel straight to the ball. Any additional movements upward, inward, or outward will cause the hitter to be late.

Once the hands are cocked back in the launch position, they fire down and forward to start the swing. But if instead they move back and upward, your swing has a "double-cock," and you are in trouble.

To gain a better understanding of what a double-cock looks like, picture a batter in his stance. His chest and midsection are facing you and his hands are inside his back shoulder. As his hands go back, they move outside his rear shoulder. Then, his hands go up (toward the sky) before dropping as he begins his swing.

If you were to draw a line simulating the correct path of the hands during their pre-swing movement, it would travel straight back with a very slight upward curve at the end. But with a double-cock, the line would look like a fishhook. That extra hook at the end of the line will cause major problems for a hitter.

Unfashionably Late

Simply put, a double-cock makes you late to the ball. The additional movement disrupts timing and lengthens your swing, causing the barrel to arrive late to the hitting zone. At the time your hands should be moving down and forward to the ball, they're moving in the wrong direction, up and back. Pitches you should drive into the outfield gap are now missed or fouled off.

Double-cocking also diminishes your power. For example, while your hands double-cock, your brain calculates that your barrel is going to be late. It then sends a message to your body to make an adjustment to compensate for the lost time. You will feel the compensation in your swing and see it manifested in your poor results.

If the pitch is an inside strike, you must make contact out in front of the plate. Because a double-cock delays your swing, the barrel now can't get to the ball in time. To counteract, you'll make an unhealthy adjustment. You'll pull your arms in close to your body and allow your bottom hand to lead the swing. Instead of getting extension and firing the barrel at the ball, you now push the barrel to the ball. This could become a habit—a bad one. A pitch that you normally pull with power is now softly served to the opposite field.

No Rhythm—No Harmony

Your timing and weight shift are also affected by the double-cock. Once the stride foot plants (and you're committed to swinging), the hips start rotating and your weight begins to transfer forward. Because the hands are lagging behind, the power from your hip torque and weight transfer are diminished. Instead of a rhythmic, powerful swing, your mechanics become choppy—the hands never get in synch—and without their natural flow.

So how do you eliminate this potential disaster? Think of the swing as a movement broken into two parts—straight back and fire. Move the hands back on a straight line, and then fire the bat directly to the ball. Think of moving your hands from point A to point B to point C. Point A being the stance position, point B being the launch position, and point C being the incoming baseball.

Have a coach or teammate watch your hands to make sure they're not moving back and upward. If the double-cock is ingrained in your muscle memory, it may be a tough habit to break. Follow the drills below to help retrain your pre-swing movement. Remember, straight back and fire. Straight back and fire.

> "At times, guys will gear up too much for their swing. You want to move your hands back and let the ball get to you, but if you allow it to get too far into your kitchen, you're going to have trouble getting the barrel on the ball. Moving the hands up or too far back doesn't allow you enough time to get to the ball."
> — *Charles Johnson*

DRILL 1

■ With a coach or teammate standing behind you, take your batting stance. Flatten the bat out in your hands so it's pointed at the umpire. Holding the bat in this position will allow you to feel the hands moving straight back instead of up. If the end of the bat begins to point toward the sky, you know your hands are moving upward.

Now, with the bat in the flat position, stride and move your hands back. As your hands near the launch position, allow your coach or teammate to grab hold of the barrel. After pausing for a short time, your partner should yell, "Swing!" Swing the bat from that position. Repeat ten times and move on to Drill 2.

DRILL 2

■ Using a batting tee, break your swing down into two parts. Instead of striding and swinging in one continuous motion, pause after separation. Feel the hands cocked and in the proper position. Then, fire the barrel from this position to the ball. A coach should call out, "Back . . . Fire!" It is important for the coach or teammate to make sure your hands move directly to the ball from the launch position.

If the hands still move upward toward your ear, exaggerate the movement backward. Push your hand back toward the catcher's mask and fire from that position. Even if it feels odd, chances are you're firing from the correct position. Repeat fifteen times and move on to Drill 3.

DRILL 3

■ Take live batting practice with the pitcher throwing from approximately 20 feet. Again, focus on your hands and their pre-swing movement. Think about the swing being two parts—*straight back and fire*. If you begin to feel "long" to the ball, you may be double-cocking again. Go back to the tee and take some more swings. Repeat fifteen times and go back to Drill 1 for a second circuit.

Fault #20 Tucking Your Hands into Your Body

The swing technique of pulling your hands in, closer to your body, is extremely useful when you're trying to get around on an inside pitch, when you're trying to get the barrel of the bat on the ball, and when you're trying to avoid getting jammed. Yet this same technique, when used to hit pitches in the other parts of the strike zone, is a major fault.

Tucking the hands in will produce a swing void of power and quickness. The hands are not given enough freedom to generate maximum force and speed. Also, the hips will sway (as shown) instead of quickly rotatoing. The barrel is then "pushed" to the ball instead of "fired."

Avoid a Power Outage—Get the Hands in and the Barrel out in Front

The first sign of this fault is a serious power outage; that is, an inability to drive pitches into the power alleys and over the fence. Instead, it's likely that your tucked hand position is producing short, lifeless fly balls weakly flared over the infield. These occur with frequency when you're not getting your arms extended properly, one of the sources of hitting power.

Pulling in your arms gets the barrel to the ball but it diminishes the speed at which the barrel of the bat is traveling. When you fail to extend your arms, you shorten the arc of the barrel of the bat. A shortened arc produces lower speeds, and bat speed is the single most significant factor in producing hard-hit balls. It's true that your trunk and hips can rotate just as quickly with a shortened arc, but the rotation cannot overcome the shortened arc of the bat and thus accelerate the bat to its maximum speed.

Albert Belle doesn't allow his hands to get trapped. He moves them straight to the ball and makes solid contact.

Limited Wrist Snap

When you tuck in your arms, you also limit the uncocking of the wrists, the action that produces the palm up, palm down position at contact; this also slows the speed of the bat. If you snap your wrists to the normal palm up, palm down position while pulling in your arms you would take the bat decisively off the prescribed plane of approach to the ball. If you were lucky enough to make contact with such a maneuver, you'd only be able to pull a weakly hit ball into foul territory.

The desired movement of the lead arm is a two-levered chop delivered at impact of the ball with the bat. The first lever is the arm swinging from the shoulder socket forward. Just before it reaches rigidity it swings from the elbow and locks in the palm up, palm down position. Pitchers throw hard pitches inside to prevent this extension and thus rob you of power. You must try to reach this position to achieve maximum power; employ the tucked or arms-pulled-in position, in which the arms are not fully extended, only when fighting off a two-seam, cut, or tailing fastball that is boring inside.

DRILL

■ This is a three-part exercise that focuses on getting full extension, especially on the inside pitch. You'll need a regulation home plate and a hanging tire or other object that will allow you to strike it with a bat without causing harm to your hands or arms. For the first drill, you need only the plate and some balls.

STEP 1

Take your normal stance but choke up on the bat 3 to 4 inches. Then straighten the left arm while pushing the bat handle backward and pointing the end of the barrel of the bat toward the pitcher. Your left arm should be absolutely straight, not bending at the elbow. Your lead shoulder should be tucked under your chin and you should feel a pulling across your back and upper shoulder.

Don't be concerned that the position feels somewhat uncomfortable—this is a drill, not your new stance.

Next, have someone soft-toss twenty-five to thirty balls into the middle and outer portion of the strike zone. Keeping your left arm straight from the starting point to just past contact, swing and hit the balls. This will give you the feeling of full extension, which is the goal even when producing a swing that starts by tucking or pulling in your arms.

STEP 2

Take your normal stance, choking up 6 to 8 inches (at the top of the handle). Make sure you choke up enough so that you can easily manipulate the weight of the barrel. Stand in front of the hanging tire. Position yourself in relationship to the tire so that upon impact the bat is square to the tire, or perpendicular to an imaginary pitch. Remove your top hand and strike the tire as if it were a pitch waiting to be hit. Use a short, powerful chopping action. Uncoil your hips and torso. Rotate the shoulders. Try to drive the bat through the tire.

Start with fifteen to twenty repetitions a session and slowly increase to fifty, adding five each time. After fifteen sessions, add the top hand and repeat. Continue until you feel you have ingrained this move—the short, powerful, and direct path from the launch position to the ball—into your approach to the ball. This will help you shorten and accelerate the path you need to take to the ball, and it will also strengthen your hands, wrists, forearms, and shoulders.

Next, reposition the tire so that the location of your contact is 5 to 6 inches in front of the plate but within the black on the inside edge. Paint or

> "The hands should lead and stay flat through the zone. That will keep the barrel on plane with the ball. You want to be direct and hit through the ball. You don't want to move the hands in toward your body or out away from it. Do not manipulate the hands. We create a deceleration of the hands when we manipulate them, and the hips will have a tendency to sway. We don't want the hips to sway, we want them to fire."
>
> *— Hal McRae*

chalk a spot on the tire as your target. The target represents an inside strike, on the black of the plate. Swing by pulling in your hands and firing the barrel of the bat to the target. The secret is to uncoil as quickly as possible and then extend the arms as soon as the hips clear (open them, facing your belly button toward the shortstop if you're a right-handed batter). Get the barrel out in front. In a game situation, you won't always get full extension, but in this drill try to get as much as possible. Don't let the pitcher reduce or shut down your power!

STEP 3

This drill will help you recognize when you must pull in the hands to swing successfully. Go back to soft tossing but randomly move the ball around in the strike zone. Swing at twenty-five to thirty balls. On the inside pitches concentrate on getting extension of the arms by pulling in the hands, spinning the hips open, and delivering the barrel of the bat to the ball.

Fault #21 Failing to Pick Up Release Points

> "I don't think enough attention is placed on the visual aspect of hitting. I truly believe the better hitters see the ball better and see the ball longer. I think the better hitters have quicker recognition of the fastball, breaking ball, change-up, and their locations."
>
> — *Sonny Pittaro,*
> *college coach*

Develop the sweetest swing of all time and it won't be worth a dime if you're unable to see the ball early out of the pitcher's hand. What you can't see, you can't hit.

To give yourself the best chance of getting "good wood" on a pitch, you must have a clear focus on the ball as it leaves the pitcher's hand. Hitters run into two main problems when trying to accomplish this. They set their focus on the release point too early or too late.

Too Early/Too Late

Looking for and finding the release point too quickly is the most common mistake. Your eyes tire and lose focus. In some cases, you may even blink. When this happens, your chances of making contact are between slim and none.

The eyes must be fresh as the pitch is delivered. It takes approximately four-tenths of a second for the ball to get from the pitcher's hand to home plate. Your eyes have half of that time to recognize the location of the pitch and the pitch type (fastball, curveball, etc.). During that two-tenths of a second, the eyes alert the brain as to whether you should swing or not. It takes

Left: Bret Saberhagen takes his rocker step. At this point, your eyes should be in soft focus, gazing at something broad like the lettering on his jersey. *Center:* As Saberhagen begins to swing his arm upward, your eyes should shift to the point of release. *Right:* At this point, the eyes should be locked on the point of release. This is called the hard focus and necessitates your undivided attention.

the final two-tenths to physically swing the bat. Any time wasted on blinking or sharpening your focus is a lost opportunity (or pitch).

Picking up the release point too late is also problematic. When your eyes are moving to find the ball, it's difficult to focus and identify its speed and location. By the time your eyes get set and locked on the ball, it will be past you and in the catcher's glove. Your lone chance is if the pitch is off-speed, but even then it will be tough to hit the ball with authority.

Soft Center/Hard Focus

The question remains, where should I be looking and when? On every pitch, you should have what is called a soft center and a hard focus. A soft center is a general area around the pitcher where your eyes should look. Focusing on something specific will tire the eyes out too quickly.

Gaze out to a general area from the time the pitcher stands on the rubber to the early stages of his motion. Your soft center target could be the pitcher's face or his chest. Many believe even these locations to be too specific. If so, try looking at the centerfield fence area. The objective is to keep the eyes relaxed.

To practice picking up release points, there's no substitute for seeing live pitches.

"When I stuggle, I realize that I'm not seeing the ball. To fix the problem, I don't worry about where my hands are, how my feet are set up, or where my weight is. I concentrate on seeing the ball and hitting it right back up the middle."

— *Scott Rolen*

As the pitcher begins his armswing (after he breaks the ball from his glove), the eyes should shift to a hard focus. The hard focus is a concentrated stare at the pitcher's release point. The eyes must be locked on this spot to pick up the ball as soon as it's released.

By observing the pitcher during warm-ups and in the on-deck circle, you can establish the location of his release point. If you're searching for it while you're at the plate, you'll pick up the ball too late to attack it.

Varying Release Points

The pitcher's purpose is to deceive the hitter. Some are successful in accomplishing this and make a hitter's life very frustrating. New York Yankee pitchers David Cone and Orlando "El Duque" Hernandez are notorious for changing arm angles from pitch to pitch. Even more troubling is that they're able to throw any pitch from any release point, so it's not as if they're tipping off the type of pitch by changing their point of release.

Tip your cap to Cone and Hernandez for their unique capabilities, but never surrender. Use what you see during the soft focus to help anticipate the release point. When a pitcher drops down to throw sidearm, he'll first lower

Hal McRae on Being a Hitting Coach

"You have to know the individual and be able to communicate and have key phrases. I can say 'stay balanced' and the hitter will know what that means. I can say 'stay on the ball,' 'use the middle,' or 'you're too wide,' and he'll know what I mean. But I try to limit it to that. Just a few key phrases. You don't want to be going all over the map discussing things in the middle of a game. You have to know when to talk to a player, what to say, and how much you say. Some hitters are more sensitive than others.

"Understand that the hitter can't have a lot of doubt when he's going up to the plate. You have to be very careful and conscious of what you're saying in trying to help him. If you tell him too much, he's going to doubt himself when he walks up to the plate. Your job is to eliminate doubt, not create doubt. If he doubts himself, it's all over. If I see something that if brought to his attention may create some doubt, I may have to wait for a couple of days to talk to that hitter. You've always got to give things some time to work themselves out.

"The time to educate the hitter and break things down are during his soft-toss drills or in the cage. Give him one thing to work on, though. Don't give five or six different things to do because it will be counterproductive. For example, say the hitter is getting started late. Work on that and that alone. Now, you haven't confused him and he's concentrating solely on getting started on time. Once he gets it going and feels himself improving, it eliminates doubt. Now he feels like when you tell him something, it's going to help him. If you tell him too many different things and talk long, he's not going to want to listen to you."

his body by flexing his rear leg. He'll then roll his front shoulder closed (toward his throwing side) to increase the whipping action of his delivery. If you notice either of these tendencies, anticipate a lower point of release. If his upper body stays tall and his front shoulder square (pointed toward home plate), expect a three-quarters delivery.

DRILL

■ When the problem is picking up release points, there is no substitute for seeing live pitching. When a teammate (pitcher) is throwing in the bullpen or in the gym, stand up at the plate and take pitches. Focus on identifying his release point and folllow each pitch into the catcher's glove. When he begins throwing breaking balls and off-speed pitches, call out the type of pitch he throws immediately after recognition.

Paul O'Neill

Hip Rotation and Weight Transfer

The respective roles of hip rotation and weight transfer in the swing are subject to debate. Many hitting gurus encourage batters to employ significant weight shift, which is linear movement to and through the ball. Others will argue the approach should be more rotational, which is marked by explosive hip movement and not as much linear movement.

The best hitters use a little bit of both. You must have some linear movement to transfer the power from your rear side to the point of contact. You must also rotate your hips to generate greater bat speed and get the power of your lower body into your swing.

Some hitters use more weight shift while others are more rotational, but all good hitters incorporate both. Many hitters adjust their approach depending on the count. With two strikes, they'll sacrifice some power and use more weight shift to keep the bat in the hitting zone longer. Ahead in the count, good hitters "sit" on a pitch, that is, look to swing at pitches in certain areas of the strike zone, becoming more rotational, hoping to drive the ball for power.

Before analyzing faults that occur during the weight shift and rotational stages of the swing, let's first describe what should happen.

To begin, about 60 percent of your weight should rest on your rear leg when you're in your stance. As the pitcher begins his delivery, you coil away from the pitcher, generating backward momentum. (As you'll read several times in this book, you must go back before you move forward.) That slight momentum or weight shift, however, should never go outside your rear leg. It must stay inside your rear leg to keep your head and eyes locked on the pitch.

Just before the pitch is released, you separate; that is, your front foot strides forward as your hands push back to the launch position. Your stride foot lands with the leg slightly bent. Your weight begins to shift forward, a controlled linear movement toward the point of contact. Your front leg stiffens, and your hips rotate as you fire the barrel to the ball.

The amount of hip rotation is determined by the location of the pitch. On an inside strike, the hips rotate fully. If you're a right-handed hitter, the hips will face the area between the shortstop and pitcher. On pitches over the middle, the hips rotate less and will face the pitcher. On balls thrown to the outside corner, you generate minimal hip rotation and the hips will face the area between the second baseman and pitcher.

Several faults will be discussed in this section. Young hitters often fail to rotate their hips and swing the bat with just their arms. When swinging at breaking pitches, hitters often shift their weight forward of their front leg and hit off their front foot. Some hitters rotate too soon while others rotate too much.

This section of the book may be the least glamorous but most important for self-improvement. Using the torso and your lower body can transform you from a weak hitter into a dangerous hitter. Much as with the golf swing, weight transfer and hip torque fuel the swing. Take a look at Tiger Woods. Why does he hit the ball so hard and far? The answer lies in his balanced weight shift and explosive hip torque. These factors are important to any powerful swinging motion, be it golf or baseball.

> "There has to be a happy medium between weight shift and rotation, a combination of the two. If there is no weight shift, you become too rotational and you can't handle off-speed or pitches away. If you don't rotate, you'll lose power and bat speed and become vulnerable to hard pitches inside."
>
> — *Dave Gallagher, college coach and professional hitting instructor*

Fault #22 Little or No Weight Transfer

Proper batting technique includes a coordination of coiling and uncoiling of the hips with a nearly simultaneous shifting of the weight from the back side (rear leg) to the front side (front leg). Much has been written—but less unanimously agreed upon—about the respective roles of these two actions in mastering the art and science of hitting. Ted Williams emphasized the rotation of the hips and the late Charley Lau felt that a weight shift was critical in achieving a good batting stroke. In the end, however, both play major roles in successfully hitting a baseball. You must shift your weight from the rear leg to a stiff front leg, and you must rotate your hips to build sufficient speed of the hands and bat when striking the ball.

Shifting the Load: Weight Back, Weight Forward

When it comes to the issue of transferring weight during the swing, a fine line separates a fault from a correct technique. For example, a player who simply lifts his stride foot and replants it where it started employs minimal weight shift and maximum hip rotation. Nomar Garciaparra, an American League batting champion, is a good example of this style of hitting. He lifts the heel of his stride foot and drops it as he begins his hip rotation and swing.

With no weight transfer forward, the upper body falls back and away from the ball. There is no energy transmitted to and through the ball. The hitter will often fall off-balance in his follow-through.

Does he have the fault of failing to shift his weight? Not really, because his technique is not entirely devoid of a weight shift. No swing is. His weight shifts from his back leg to this front leg when he drops his heel. His transfer of weight onto the front leg is accomplished with very little forward motion of his torso and upper body and almost no forward motion of his lower body.

With this unique style, Nomar is very quickly "in business," that is, ready to rotate his hips and launch the bat toward the pitch. Some believe that his batting style (of lifting and dropping the heel of his stride foot while keeping it in place) is a split-second faster than a batter who picks up his front foot and strides toward the pitcher. Yes, it's true that Garciaparra exhibits an unusual (and extraordinarily efficient) weight transfer, but his batting style is not faulty, and it certainly does not need any fixing.

Don't Reverse Pivot

Those faults that are associated with little or no weight transfer more often occur when a batter fails to follow the proper sequence of first going back, or loading the rear side, then shifting the weight onto the front leg. In a proper weight shift, the front leg stiffens like a post, allowing the batter to use this firm front side as a base for his hip rotation. A faulty weight shift most often occurs when a player reverses the shift, that is, moves his weight prematurely to the front side and then moves it back onto the rear leg to swing. This fault is similar to the fault of reverse pivoting found in golfers.

If you have this fault, you're probably hitting a lot of pop-ups (you will be dropping your rear shoulder as you clear your other side out of the way of your arms and hands). Other sure signs of this fault are (1) your balance is poor, often falling backward on a missed swing; (2) you have trouble tracking pitches due to head movement that carries the eyes away from the hitting zone; (3) your front foot leaves the ground in the follow-through (if any foot lifts off the ground during the follow-through of the swing, it would be the rear foot of a hitter who uses a pronounced weight shift style of hitting, which allows the weight to be transferred onto the front foot).

The self-toss drill will help you feel the importance of weight transfer in your swing. Get into your stance and hold a ball in your top hand. Flip the ball straight up over home plate (toss it up between 1 and 2 feet), and hit through the ball to center field. Notice the weight transferring forward into the ball *(right)*. To practice inside pitches, toss the ball out in front of your stride foot. To practice outside pitches, toss the ball off your back hip. Remember to keep that front shoulder closed.

DRILL

■ A good way to get the feel of shifting your weight properly is to hit balls tossed to yourself with a fungo bat. If you don't have a fungo bat, use a regular bat. In this exercise, first take your normal position in the batter's box. Next rock back onto the rear leg as you toss the ball in the air in front of you, then rock onto the front leg as you swing and hit the ball. When rocking back, turn your hips slightly toward the rear. When rocking over onto the front foot, turn your hips so your belt buckle is facing the direction of the target. These movements simulate the weight shift that must be a part of your regular swings at pitches thrown in a game.

Add bat control and directional hitting to this drill by tossing the ball over different parts of the plate. To hit a ball up the middle, toss the ball over the center of the plate just back of your front foot. To pull the ball, toss the ball over the inside corner of the plate slightly forward of your stride foot. To hit balls to the opposite field, toss balls on the outside of the plate just forward of your rear foot. Throughout this drill concentrate on keeping your front shoulder closed as you approach the ball.

A good way to practice this is to get a teammate to catch fifty to sixty ground balls, then have your buddy hit the same number of grounders to you.

Fault #23 Little or No Hip Rotation

Encountering an aspiring hitter who exhibits absolutely no rotation of the hips is highly unlikely. The body's natural reaction to swinging anything—an ax, a stick, a racket—from point A, say the right shoulder area, to Point B, the left shoulder area, would automatically engage the hips in a coiling and/or uncoiling movement around the spine. What is more common among batters having difficulty, however, is a restricted rotation of the hips.

The Missing Link: Hip Rotation

Beginning players, especially at the T-ball and Little League levels, often exhibit this flaw in their swings. The upper body and arms dominate their swings. The legs and hips remain as stationary as possible while the arms and hands travel with the bat toward the target, the pitched ball or ball set on a tee.

The causes of this swing are often rooted in the fear of not being able to make contact with the ball. Thus, players who inhibit their rotation of the

Left: With little or no hip rotation, the hitter lacks power and quickness because his major muscles (the legs, buttocks, and torso) are dormant. *Right:* Rotating the hips generates greater bat speed and power.

"For me, the lower body is where all my power comes from. If I get a good hip turn, that's when I get the most bat speed coming through the zone. The rest is just hand-eye coordination and making good contact."

— Will Clark

hips often succeed in hitting the ball, their primary objective, but without delivering any appreciable force to the ball. In other words, they make contact but the ball goes nowhere. Instead, these swings produce weak grounders and pop-ups. They have failed to generate a swing with a sufficient speed of the barrel to drive the ball on a line through or up in the air over the infield.

Here are a few signs of poor hip rotation. Check these swing mechanics to see if you're suffering from this affliction.

1. The belt buckle points toward opposite field foul territory instead of toward the pitcher upon conclusion of the swing.
2. The rear shoulder remains to the rear of the chin throughout the swing (in a proper swing, the rear shoulder is pulled around the spine toward the front of the body, eventually passing forward of the chin).
3. The legs do not flex, and the rear knee remains rigid (in a proper swing the rear knee flexes, creating an angle of approximately 90 degrees at the knee joint).
4. The follow-through of the arms and bat stops almost immediately after contact with the ball.

Ken Griffey Jr. fires his hips with a controlled weight shift, sending this pitch a lot further than the pitcher had hoped.

These signs may also be showing up in your plate appearance in games. Hitting weak ground balls (inability to drive the ball through or over the infielders) and difficulty in getting the barrel of the bat on inside pitches (instead, you're hitting the ball off the sweet spot toward the handle) point to lack of hip rotation.

Restricted hip rotation is often a direct result of a closed stride (see page 44). If you stride toward home plate, you will be unable to fully rotate your hips. The pitcher will dominate you with inside fastballs.

DRILL 1

■ Hold a bat behind your back a few inches above your waistline (see page 88). The bat should be pointed north to south (or knob at the pitcher). Take a short, controlled stride and rotate your hips. As you fire your hips, keep the weight of your upper body over the point of contact. In the finished position, your belt buckle faces the pitcher, head looking down over the plate, and the bat is pointed east to west.

"When you rotate, it makes your hands quicker and allows you to drive the ball with more power because we're hitting the ball with the biggest muscles in our body— the lower back, the butt, the thighs, and the hips."

— *Hal McRae*

Place a bat behind your back and assume your stance. Take your stride and fire your hips open so your belly button faces the pitcher. Finish in a balanced position with your head looking down at the point of contact.

DRILL 2

■ Here is a drill to help you master proper hip rotation. Stick a towel in your pants directly over your belt buckle (covering your belly button). Take your batting stance without a bat, hands on hips, letting the towel hang below your knees and between your legs. Next, bend your legs slightly, as you would when taking the "athletic position," that is, keep the weight on the balls and inside of the feet, legs flexed. You're ready to practice a hip rotation.

Push down with the ball of the rear foot and spin the foot inward toward an imaginary pitcher. Simultaneously, push forward on the rear hip with the hand that rests on the hip; keep turning the hips until the belt buckle faces the pitcher.

If you have rotated correctly the towel should be resting over the lead leg, covering the knee. The front foot has remained closed, that is, pointed perpendicular to the rear foot, and the rear leg has flexed at the knee, forming a 90-degree angle. This knee has moved into the space where the towel was hanging prior to rotation of the hips.

After you are able to repeatedly do this successfully, place a bat in your hands and practice the rotation without a ball. You'll find that your rotation has added speed to the forward motion of the hands, and that your hands have moved beyond the finishing point of a swing with a restricted hip rotation. Now you're ready to add the ball. Try it on a tee first, and then have someone pitch to you. A proper hip rotation will definitely put some pop in your bat.

Fault #24 **Premature Hip Rotation**

Hip rotation and uncoiling of the torso are vital elements in generating maximum force. A golf swing, a tennis swing, a shot put throw, a right-cross in boxing—all of them require hip rotation and uncoiling of the torso.

Hitting a baseball is no different. Rotating the hips increases both bat speed and power. But if the hips rotate prematurely, your swing loses the explosiveness or power created by your legs and torso. The hips must lead the swing, but just barely.

Left: The front hip has opened early, pulling the front shoulder and hands away from the incoming pitch. This sacrifices power and the ability to handle the outside strike. *Right:* The front hip remains closed. The hitter's energy is stored and balanced over home plate.

Taking batting practice from short range can help develop your timing and rhythm.

Think Rhythmic—Not Robotic

One cause of this problem stems from careless instruction. By trying to fix one problem, coaches create another one. Here's how. At a young age, hitters commonly fail to rotate their hips. In an attempt to incorporate the hitter's hips into his swing, coaches often isolate hip rotation by breaking down the swing into three parts—stride, rotate hips, swing. They execute drills off of tees and soft toss, having hitters take a robotic approach. Coaches will call out, "Stride—hips—swing!"

In theory, the coach is correct in emphasizing the importance of hip rotation. But in reality, the pupil may begin to develop bad habits. The hitter can become too mechanical and lose fluidity and quickness. Through repetitious training, he may take his stride and open his hips as the pitcher releases the ball, exaggerating the time between the uncoiling of the hips and the swing. The lower and upper body will not be synchronized, and the swing will suffer immensely.

Premature hip rotation diminishes bat speed and power. You will have difficulty keeping your front shoulder from pulling out early and, consequently, will be unable to handle outside strikes. Last, your back shoulder may dip by trying to keep your bat in the hitting zone longer. Because your hips open up early, your hands will also be pulled in that direction. Dipping the back shoulder will drop the barrel of the bat below a level plane.

To better understand the pitfalls of premature hip rotation, grab a bat and take your stance at the plate. Take your stride and rotate your hips, but keep your hands back in the launch position. Now ask the pitcher to throw you a pitch. You don't have very much left to swing with, do you? Although this is exaggerated, it's not far off from what you'll experience in the game.

Smoothness and Tempo Promote Quickness

The baseball swing, much like the golf swing, should be rhythmic. The lower and upper body separate during the stride, but they fire through the hitting zone nearly simultaneously. The hips do lead the hands slightly, but the movement is concurrent. Pure rotational hitters emit a more violent movement, but the hips and hands are synchronized. When the hips rotate too far in front of the hands, the hands move forward; strength and speed are lost.

San Francisco Giants manager Dusty Baker installed speakers in the batting cages for his players. He feels playing music during batting practice relaxes hitters and helps them maintain rhythm. This not only helps cure a swing that is too mechanical but eliminates tension as well.

One other point of reference to check: make sure your front foot is closed when taking your stride (toe perpendicular to the pitcher). If your stride foot lands open (toe pointed toward the pitcher), your hips will open with it. Keep your front foot closed and the hips will follow suit.

> "My slumps are usually caused by pulling off the ball too early. My hips and front shoulder fly open too soon. If this is happening to you, you've got to trust your hands, let the ball get back to you, and try to hit it back through the middle."
>
> — *Mike Lieberthal*

DRILL 1

■ Premature hip rotation is often caused by focusing too much attention on explosive hip rotation. Hitters become overly conscious of firing their hips. To counter, take swings off of short toss (approximately 20 feet) without trying to rotate your hips. Simply allow the weight of the bat and rhythm of your swing to open your hips naturally. In most cases, you'll find that your hips rotate (with force) without any conscious effort.

DRILL 2

■ Take short batting practice at 70 percent effort. Focus on developing rhythm between your hips and hands, and firing them through the hitting zone simultaneously. Before taking swings, visualize the rhythm of a golf or tennis swing.

Once you increase your swing speed to 100 percent, hit the first ten balls to the opposite field. This keeps you from opening your hips prematurely.

Fault #25 Over-Rotating

Spin-Outs at the Plate Can Crash Your BA

An over-rotated swing, although an uncommon fault, can bring your batting average crashing down. Usually, this flaw shows up in the swing of a dead pull hitter. Recall the corkscrew swings of baseball Hall of Fame slugger Reggie Jackson or modern day, left-handed power-hitter Brian Giles. Sluggers like Jackson and Giles, who have swings that border on over-rotation, rely on tremendous agility and strength—especially in the lower body—to maintain their balance as they spin in the batter's box. The styles of Jackson and Giles are similar to that of the greatest slugger of all—Babe Ruth, who fully rotated but didn't lower his body into the ground as much. Ruth spun his hips and body more like a top; Jackson twisted like a pretzel. But these players were successful with their extreme rotations because they were exceptionally gifted. The average player would be hard pressed to copy their styles and be successful.

The hitter rotates his hips too far and spins off and away from the ball.

Hip rotation should be explosive, yet controlled. Here, the hitter maintains balance over home plate in a good follow through position.

Letting It Fly

Rotation of the hips and shoulders is part of every swing. A full rotation—that is, the front shoulder finishes in the position of the rear shoulder, and the rear shoulder finishes in the position of the front shoulder (a rotation of 180 degrees)—is almost always restricted to hitting an inside pitch. However, it's not uncommon for a batter to fully rotate on a pitch "right down Broadway," one that's over the center of the plate at the height preferred by the batter. This is what is often termed "sitting on a pitch." This is when a batter anticipates and looks for a certain pitch, say a fastball, in a certain area—such as middle of the plate to inside off the middle an inch or two—and then seemingly "sits down" and rotates fully at the precise spot where he needs to be to meet the ball. Drives that leave the ballpark are often the result.

Full rotations, however, seldom occur when hitting an outside strike. The key to hitting pitches over the middle and outside of the plate is to rotate the hips less than 90 degrees, and the shoulders less than 180 degrees. For a right-handed batter this is when the belt buckle ends up facing to the right of the pitcher toward the second baseman. The batter's task is to keep the bat on the plane that is necessary for meeting the ball squarely and to drive the ball into the opposite field, hands leading the barrel in the impact zone.

"You've got to let the ball travel back deep in order to hit the outside strike. That's the first order of business. You've got to throw your hands at the inside part of the baseball, rather than the outside part of the ball. When you get your hands around the outside of the ball, that's when you pull that weak ground ball to the infield. Personally, I try not to swing at outside strikes unless I have two strikes on me."

— *Jay Bell*

Power hitters, like Phillies star Pat Burrell, often rotate too far and pull off the ball.

How to Spot Over-Rotation

Over-rotation is a flaw that can be recognized immediately. Your shoulders move more than 180 degrees during the swing. You consistently lose balance, falling backward and away from home plate. Your head faces foul ground at the finish of the swing. You lose track of the ball's path (eyes and head move too much).

If you're over-rotating, your ball-contact pattern may show one or more of the following characteristics.

1. No contact on pitches outside in the strike zone
2. Inconsistent contact with pitches in middle of strike zone
3. Fair balls are always pulled, no opposite field hits
4. Inside strikes are always pulled into foul territory

Because over-rotating pulls your head off the ball, it positions the body at a disadvantage when attempting to hit pitches over the outside of the plate. Your moving eyes cannot track and calculate the trajectory of the pitch. The movement away from the center of the plate limits your coverage. Any batting

Tee work is the time to fine-tune your mechanics.

movement that limits your coverage of the plate and at the same time hampers sighting the ball is going to lead to a string of "0-fers." For right-handed batters, it leaves you in a difficult position for starting your run toward first base. An over-rotated swing will pull you farther from your intended path and cause you to temporarily lose balance. The split-second you may need to leg out a hit is gone!

DRILLS

■ Here are two drills that can help give you the proper rotation.

1. Using a batting tee, place the ball slightly forward of the front or striding foot. Swing at the ball and maintain focus on the empty tee after striking the ball. Rotate fully and maintain balance. This drill will give you a good rotation but keep the rear shoulder from traveling too far forward.
2. Using the soft-toss method, place a ball on the ground slightly forward of the stride foot. Soft-toss the ball over the ball on the ground. Hit the ball

as it passes over the ball on the ground. Follow through while maintaining focus on the ball on the ground. Keep your balance throughout.

Fault #26 Shifting Your Weight Outside Your Front Leg

When you fall away to the outside (toward foul territory) upon completion of the swing, you're shifting your weight incorrectly. You're letting your weight roll away from the axis of your body. This topples you away from the hitting zone, causing a breakdown in proper mechanics.

Poor Balance Fosters Poor Mechanics

"I'm 6'3" and have a lot of leverage so I'm able to get out on my front foot, but maintain control of my weight shift. Often hitters who try to do this get too far out on their front foot and shift their weight forward incorrectly. This will result in a lot of weak ground balls."

— *Alex Rodriguez*

The fault of shifting your weight outside your front leg is really a fault of poor balance during the swing. Both the weight-shift and rotational systems of hitting require the front leg to brace and allow the hips and torso to uncoil into it. However, with the rotational swing, the rear leg stays in contact with the ground throughout, thus better stabilizing the batter's side-to-side balance and helping to eradicate the chances of acquiring this fault.

If you are shifting your weight outside your front leg you're also going to be losing your balance. There may be several causes for this; here are the more common ones.

Bracing the Front Leg

The most common cause is the failure to brace the front leg properly. As the weight moves forward from the back side to the front side during the swing, the front leg braces, that is, it becomes a post around and into which the torso and hips rotate. If this leg does not stiffen, the momentum of the weight shift brings the weight forward and to the outside of the plant foot. The result will be loss of balance and a powerless swing.

Another mechanical cause is the continual movement forward of the top half of the body. This forces the leg to flex in an effort to control the weight that is passing forward of the knee and plant foot. This flaw is more common among batters who favor the weight-shift style of hitting.

A third cause is failing to uncoil into the front leg. This flaw begins with the stance of the early part of the swing when the batter fails to close or square the hips. Without a coiling or closing of the hips, the only way to build momentum is to make a vigorous shift toward the pitcher. With the hips already pointing away from the centerline toward the pitcher, the shift

Left: Allowing your weight to leak outside your front leg can lead to some futile swings. *Right:* A good swing thought is to "stay behind the ball." That will keep you from shifting your weight over your front side.

takes the weight outside the axis of the body (imaginary vertical line extending from head to feet via the spine). Again, the result is loss of balance and poor hand speed (no power).

Stay over the Ball

Players also lose balance and improperly shift their weight to the heels when they "stand up"—that is, raise up their entire body during the swing—or pull their head and upper body away from the centerline toward the pitcher.

When you move the swing away from the body's axis, which is what you're doing when you shift toward the outside of the centerline between you and the pitcher, you lose the ability to generate hip, shoulder, arm and hand speed. Result? Diminished capacity to track pitches and, when you do make contact, no pop in your bat.

Players who "stand up" out of their swings or pull their heads and upper body out too early will have a habitual case of "0-fers" (no hits, 0 for 3, 0 for 4, etc.). They won't be able to hit because they've shifted their weight

Andruw Jones carries his upper body out over his front side. He's left with relatively no strength to drive the ball. Although Jones attempts to keep his weight back by stiffening his front leg, his rear leg collapses, allowing his upper body to lunge forward. As a result, he weakly chops the ball to third base.

improperly to their heels and lost the athleticism—balance and agility—that is necessary for moving into and attacking the pitch.

DRILL

■ Practice this in front of a mirror. Take your normal stance, then take your stride. Place a sawed-off broomstick or other long stick in the ground alongside your front or leading hip (left hip for a right-handed batter). The stick should be 1 to 2 inches to the side of your hip, just enough for you to rotate without touching it.

Take your stride and swing and check to see that your rotation does not touch the broomstick. Repeat twenty-five times.

Another drill is to pay attention to your "takes" during batting practice. Have the pitcher mix in random pitches out of the strike zone. After the pitch goes by, check your balance and weight distribution. Then make adjustments accordingly. Have a coach or someone who knows proper hitting mechanics watch you and help with your checking and adjustments.

Why Can't I Hit a Curveball?

Are you a great hitter until the pitcher starts breaking off deuces? If so, you're not alone. Most hitters would much rather hit a fastball. It's easier to hit something that's traveling on a straight line.

The first step to hitting a breaking pitch is identifying it. When you recognize the pitch is a breaking ball, your eyes tell your brain to keep your weight and hands back because the pitch will be traveling at a lower velocity than a fastball.

Identifying Breaking Pitches

How do you recognize a breaking ball? Well, the spin of a breaking pitch is completely different than the spin of a fastball. Fastballs roll off the pitcher's fingertips, creating a backward rotation. A breaking ball has forward rotation because the pitcher cocks his wrist and snaps it forward when releasing the pitch. Pitches such as sliders and sidearm curveballs spin sideways (or diagonal) and break on a horizontal plane.

Once you've identified the pitch, you still have to hit it. Here are a few tips that will make you a better breaking ball hitter.

- **Swing where the pitch *will* be, not where you see it.** Calculate the pitch's break and adjust your swing. (Recognizing what type of breaking ball and how much break is information you should gather while waiting on deck and watching the pitcher warm up.) If the pitch appears to be thigh-high, it will probably cross the plate around your knees. Adjust to the break or you'll swing over the pitch.
- **Shorten your swing.** The shorter the swing, the longer you can wait to commit your hands. Long swings must be initiated as the pitch is released. You have to decide the location of your swing as soon as you see the ball. Shorten your swing and you'll increase the time you have to see the pitch.
- **Look to hit the ball to the opposite field.** Because of the decreased velocity, hitters often try to pull

breaking pitches, thereby making contact too far out in front of the plate. This produces weak ground balls to the pull-side, or infield pop-ups. If you tell yourself to hit the ball to the opposite field, this will keep you on the ball longer, lock your front shoulder in, and allow you to hit breaking pitches with authority.

One other strategic note: If it's early in an at bat, or you're ahead in the count, don't swing at any breaking balls (unless they're hangers). You'll find that pitchers frequently miss the strike zone with curveballs, because it's not just a hard pitch to hit, it's a hard pitch to consistently throw for strikes. Besides, why swing at a pitch you struggle with unless you have to?

Here is what major league third baseman Scott Rolen has to say about hitting breaking balls:

"The most important element to hitting a breaking ball is letting it get to you. It's much easier said than done. You hear people all the time saying, 'Stay back, stay back,' but it's difficult to do if you're looking at a fastball. The bottom line is it's not that easy to hit a breaking ball. You can put yourself in a position to hit a breaking ball as best you can, and I do that by looking for a fastball on the outer half of the plate. If I look for a fastball in, I'm going to be too quick to open up and won't be able to wait long enough for an off-speed pitch. I look for a pitch away because you naturally have to wait longer on a pitch away.

"The other key is that I try to make the breaking ball be up to hit it. Breaking balls down and away, you're not supposed to hit those pitches. Those are pitcher's pitches. The idea is not to swing at them. Attack the breaking balls that are up, ones that are hanging a little bit, ones that are more middle-in. The ones down and away you should leave. If you have two strikes, you have to try to do something. Maybe spoil the pitch by fouling it off, but unless you have two strikes on you, leave that pitch alone."

1999 National League MVP Chipper Jones demonstrates his all-star form at the plate. He uses a toe-tap *(facing page, top right)* to load his weight back and initiates his pre-swing movement. Jones moves his hands back far beyond his rear shoulder *(this page, top right)*, an adjustment he made entering the 1999 season to generate more power from the right-hand side. This pitch is inside, so he pulls his hands in *(facing page, bottom left)* to get the barrel of the bat on the ball. Because he's unable to achieve full extention *(this page, bottom right)*, his follow-through is slightly cut off.

Will Clark

The Swing

Swinging the bat is the meat and potatoes of the hitting process. As former American League batting champion Tony Oliva put it, "It don't mean a thing if you ain't got that swing."

Do you have to own a sweet-looking swing like Junior Griffey to make it as a hitter? Fortunately, the answer is no. Not too many swing the bat with the power and smoothness of Ken Griffey Jr.

To be successful, your swing must be efficient and repeatable—you have to have everything in the right place at the right time as many times as possible. It doesn't always matter how you get it there. But assuming your pre-swing movements are not flawed, if the hands are in the palm up, palm down position, arms slightly bent as they move to extension, head down on the ball, and barrel of the bat on the fat part of the ball, you'll hit your fair share of line drives and long balls.

Another Junior, Cal Ripken, is the perfect example of a hitter whose swing works despite being less than perfect. Ripken has never been regarded as a sweet swinger. He sort of slings the bat through the hitting zone. Throughout his career, he has made countless adjustments to his stance and pre-swing movements. His determination and experimentation have paid off. He gets the barrel of the bat on the ball with consistency—consistent enough to compile over 3,000 hits and 400 home runs in the major leagues.

Picking Out Swing Faults

When you're trying to locate a problem in your swing, ask a coach or teammate to keep a watchful eye. Have him keep track of your timing. Is it early or late? This will give you a start to locating the problem. Ask him to watch your swing path from the side (facing you) where it's easier to see what's happening. The swing path should start forward and down, level off through the hitting zone, and then gradually ascend into your follow-through.

Also, it's beneficial to have your swing evaluated from behind the catcher. An onlooker can watch to see where the swing path travels in relation to home plate. Does it stay over and through home plate, or does it pull away from home plate?

A swing fault may just require a little tweaking. Perhaps your top hand or bottom hand becomes too dominant and you have to lighten up on the throttle with that hand. Maybe you're swinging with just your arms and not allowing the wrists to help fire the barrel of the bat. You don't always have to reinvent the wheel to fix your swing. You just may have to smooth out a few rough edges.

Your goal is to develop a quick, short, powerful stroke. Quickness is accomplished by staying relaxed and being tension-free. Staying short to the ball allows you to see the pitch as long as possible while letting the ball get into the hitting zone closer to your body (where your power is). The power comes from the combination of your legs, torso, forearms, and hands all exploding at the same time at the point of contact. Long swings do not produce long hits. Timely, explosive swings send balls screaming off the bat.

Once you've worked out the quirks and can generate a quick, compact, and forceful swing, practice it over and over again. You must ingrain the correct technique, make it part of your muscle memory. That way, you no longer think about swinging the bat correctly, you "just do it."

The Problem Lies in the Approach

This section includes a number of swing-related mechanical faults, many of which arise as a result of poor thinking. You can often tell what a hitter is thinking just by watching his swing. A hitter who uppercuts, pulls his front shoulder out, or overswings is thinking about going deep. One who "feels" for the ball, that is, swings tentatively or haltingly, or cuts his swing short is more than likely hoping to make contact instead of attacking the pitch.

Before making major changes and adjustments, a hitter should be honest with himself in evaluating his approach. Does he see the left fielder playing shallow, then try to drive the ball over his head? Has the hitter been told dozens of times that he needs to swing down on the ball, and as a result, his barrel is traveling downward through the hitting zone? Is the hitter mired in a horrid slump so that he fails to swing the bat aggressively in fear of missing the pitch? All of these questions (and many more) should be considered when getting to the bottom of a swing fault.

Be All That YOU Can Be

Another checkpoint: Do your game swings match your body type, strength, and skills? Jim Thome is an exceptional, power-hitting first baseman. He's able to hit the ball out of any part of the ballpark at any time. It would not make sense for him to cut down his swing and pattern it after teammate Omar Vizquel, a line drive, singles hitter. Similarly, Vizquel would be foolish to pattern his swing after Thome because Omar lacks the strength to do so.

Unfortunately, hitters commonly try to do more with the bat than they're capable of doing. Rampaging egos and testosterone surges plague hitters as much as change-ups and sliders. Hitters need to stick to what they do best. Not everyone is a home run hitter, and if a line drive hitter hits a ball over the fence every once in a while, he should consider it a mistake. As the late Hall of Famer Richie Ashburn said, "I hit 29 major league home runs and after every one of them I worried that I was swinging wrong, that I wasn't staying with my normal pattern of how the strike zone was or how I was supposed to swing. My game was built around speed. I was a guy who hit a lot of singles, doubles, and triples, not home runs. I always tried to keep the bat above the ball. I didn't want to hit the ball in the air."

Fault #27 Pulling the Front Shoulder Out Early

A fundamentally sound swing is dependent upon precise mechanical movements. These movements, which must come into play in proper sequence, must be executed at the proper time. Any deviation will produce a flawed swing. Pulling your front shoulder out early is a common flaw that haunts hitters.

At separation (see page 56), you should move your hands to the rear shoulder, loaded in position to attack the ball. If your first movement is to move the front shoulder outward (toward third base for right-handed hitters, first base for left-handed hitters), then you're pulling out too early. Your front shoulder will then tilt upward, causing your hands to drop and the barrel to drag.

The front shoulder and hands should first move toward the ball. Moving away from the ball leads to many problems.

Inside Strike or Bust

Not all hitting mistakes lead to disaster at all times. For example, if you step in the bucket (see page 46) you can still hit an inside fastball with authority. But pulling the front shoulder out too early will adversely affect your ability to handle pitches elsewhere in the strike zone. A belt-high inside fastball—something that good pitchers rarely serve up—will be about the only pitch you can handle. Anything else will be either missed or hit weakly.

> "Hitting a weak fly ball to the opposite field usually means your barrel is dragging. Nine times out of ten, that's from trying to do too much with a pitch and pulling your front shoulder out early."
>
> — *Scott Rolen*

Left: When the front shoulder opens early, your timing is flawed and plate coverage limited. *Right:* The front shoulder stays closed until the hands and bat begin moving forward to the ball. This keeps the upper body in position to cover the entire plate (with power).

Listed below are by-products of pulling your front shoulder out early. Each is a symptom of a defective swing.

- Your head and eyes move with your front shoulder and pull away from the ball.
- Your hands trail your shoulders, causing the barrel to be late.
- Your swing gets too long.
- Your swing path will start *to* and then move *away from* the ball, instead of *to* and *through* the ball.
- Because your front shoulder pulls up and out, your rear shoulder will drop down, thus causing the barrel of the bat to drop.

When your front shoulder flies open early, you need to move quickly to fix the problem, or the results will be ugly: (1) you'll swing through a lot of pitches; (2) fly balls and pop-flies will come in bunches; (3) the sweet spot of the barrel will rarely find the ball; and (4) you'll have trouble putting outside strikes in play (even when you do, they'll be weakly hit).

Detecting the Fault

The results listed above should alert you that something is wrong, but you may need outside assistance to detect this fault. Ask a coach or a person familiar with your swing to watch closely.

An experienced observer may catch the problem as it occurs—the front shoulder popping out before the hands start to the ball. But this happens very quickly and isn't easily detected. Another time period to catch this problem is in the follow-through. After finishing your swing, you should be in a balanced position, right side of face (for right-handed hitter) laid against your rear shoulder. If you're falling off balance and catching your weight with your rear leg, you're probably pulling off the ball. Your midsection (chest) will face the hole between shortstop and third base, instead of correctly facing between the shortstop position and second base (for right-handed hitters).

Replacing the Shoulders

To say the front shoulder should not rotate outward at all is grossly inaccurate. The shoulders must rotate to generate maximum power, but this has to happen at the correct time. The front shoulder rotates outward with the swing, but not before it. It's moved after the hips and torso have uncoiled, not before and not simultaneously. It must be synchronized with the arms and hands.

Hall of Famer Mike Schmidt talks about "replacing the shoulders." This means that upon the completion of your swing, the rear shoulder finishes where the front shoulder began. This is critical when "turning on an inside pitch" or "sitting on a pitch," when the swing is fully rotational. If you stop short of this position, you're cutting your swing off too early. Cutting the swing short sacrifices power (see page 138).

Note: Replacing the shoulders should occur only on pitches located over the middle and inside part of the plate. On outside strikes, the hips and shoulders rotate less.

Adjusting Your Mental Approach

Some faults can be fixed by adjusting your mental approach. Simple thoughts may help you stop pulling your front shoulder out early. The first is to "let the ball get to you, and hit it back through the middle." Refrain from reaching out for the ball and trying to pull it. This will keep the front shoulder tucked in a bit longer. Do not worry about being late on inside strikes. Your natural reactions fire the hips open and accelerate your hands to get the barrel of the bat on the ball.

"If I had one swing fault to name that troubles me most it would be pulling off the ball. One way to rectify that problem is to try to drive the ball to the opposite field. You can't drive the ball the other way by pulling off."

— *Will Clark*

Left: When the front shoulder flies open, the head goes with it. Richard Hidalgo illustrates this truism. *Right:* A thrower stands behind an "L-screen" and tosses pitches to the outside part of the plate. This allows the hitter to practice hitting to the opposite field while keeping his front shoulder closed.

Another thought is to "drive your rear shoulder forward and down to the ball." This will keep the front shoulder from tilting up and out. As your swing progresses, your rear shoulder must level off, but this is a good approach to offset the flying front shoulder.

Many coaches tell their hitters to "keep your hands inside the ball." That keeps the lead arm on a path *to* the ball instead of pulling off and away from the ball. The best swings are short and direct with no wasted movements.

Last, think about keeping your upper body balanced over the point of contact. Many refer to this as "keeping your body over the ball." This keeps your shoulders level while maintaining balance throughout the swing. While hitting from a tee, think about keeping your chest over the ball as you make contact.

Remember, this is simply a thought. Your upper body will rotate through contact and finish facing the field. But this thought will keep your body on a linear plane to and through the ball.

If you're still struggling to keep the front shoulder closed, hit every ball to the opposite field in batting practice. You can't hit to the opposite field if your shoulder flies open.

DRILL

■ Set up an "L-screen" and turn it around so the straight edge of the screen stands on the throwing side. The thrower should stand behind the screen and underhand toss balls to the batter. As soon as the ball is released, the tosser should move back behind the screen.

For this drill, work specifically on pitches tossed to the outside part of the plate. Hit each pitch to the opposite field. This forces you to keep your front shoulder closed as you allow the ball to get to you. Any time a ball is pulled, you've made the mistake of pulling your front shoulder off the ball. Keep practicing until you hit ten straight balls sharply to the opposite field.

Fault #28 Uppercutting (Dropping the Back Shoulder)

The fault of uppercutting occurs when a batter creates a low-to-high path to the pitch that is angled too severely. To understand the fault, you must first understand the correct path a batter must take to an incoming pitch.

Getting the Bat on the Correct Swing Plane

The correct swing needs to travel from the launch position (bat held shoulder high or slightly above the shoulder, hands and wrists in cocked position) into the downswing along a shallow angle to a point that is directly in the path of the ball. This point is not one, single point. It is a spot in the strike zone along the bat's path at which the ball and bat collide or intersect. Its location is within the strike zone, that is, over the plate and between the bottom of the knee and just above the belt. This is where a hitter adjusts the height of his hands, gets first the knob of the bat and then the barrel of the bat on plane and then uncoils his hips, shoulders, and arms, and fires his hands and bat barrel at the ball. Whack!

Remember: Once the bat is moving along the same plane that the pitch is traveling, it needs to continue along that path through contact. To roll the top hand immediately after contact would require perfect timing on all pitches, which is virtually impossible.

Any action that creates a severely angled path from low to high, or high to low, is flawed. Uppercutting is the flaw when the bat starts below the projected path of the pitch, travels through the plane for a very short space, and then quickly moves above the plane. This uppercutting swing plane diminishes the chances of meeting the ball squarely and driving it for a long distance.

> "Swinging up at the ball for the most part will produce pop-ups and swings and misses. You want to swing down and through the ball. A perfect example of a guy who does that well is Mike Piazza. He swings down on everything and gets great backspin carry."
> — *Mike Lieberthal*

Left: Uppercutting drops the angle of the bat as it enters the hitting zone. This makes it much more difficult to achieve square contact. *Right:* Notice the difference in the rear (right shoulder). Here, it's kept up, which allows the bat to stay level through the swing.

Signs that you may be uppercutting pitches include:

1. Frequent misses, or repeatedly swinging through pitches
2. Towering pop-ups and fly balls
3. Top-spin ground balls
4. Lateness in getting the bat around
5. Trouble hitting fastballs up in the strike zone

"The key to hitting .300 is to hit as many line drives as possible. To hit a line drive you have to get a pitch up in the strike zone and stay on top of it."

— *Jay Bell*

What causes an uppercut swing? The most common source of the problem is trying to hit the ball in the air. Hitters think that to hit the ball deep, they have to "dip and jack." They drop their back shoulder and swing up at the ball to lift it. In most cases, you'll swing under the ball or hit the bottom of it, resulting in a pop-up. Hitting the top of the ball or middle will produce a ground ball or top-spin line drive. Uppercutting produces negative results that could be improved by leveling off your swing.

Kenny vs. Ken

As we advocated in *The Louisville Slugger® Ultimate Book of Hitting*, there is no single correct method of hitting. There are many factors to consider when developing the swing perfect for you, such as your size, strength, running speed, bat speed, and hand-to-eye coordination.

There are, however, several absolutes to hitting. For example, your bat should be in the launch position the moment your stride foot touches the ground. But don't alter your swing to look like someone else. If Chuck Knoblauch took the same type of swings as José Canseco, Knoblauch would quickly find himself searching for a new occupation.

Acknowledge Your Strengths and Weaknesses

It's important to address your strengths and weaknesses, then focus your efforts accordingly. Ken Griffey Jr. and Kenny Lofton are two left-handed-hitting center fielders. They're outstanding offensive players, but each employs very different and unique swings and styles.

Lofton succeeds by getting on base and utilizing his great running speed to wreak havoc on his opponents. He usually keeps the ball out of the air and gets on base any way he can. Lofton employs a short, level swing to put the ball in play consistently. Although he is capable of hitting the ball out of the ballpark, Lofton serves his team best as a spark plug or tablesetter. He occasionally leaves the yard, but in most cases, it's a mistake.

Griffey is a great home run hitter. He can change the course of the game with one swing and looks to elevate the ball into the outfield bleachers. Griffey has such tremendous hand speed and hand-to-eye coordination that he can increase his shoulder turn and generate a longer, more powerful swing. This increases his strikeout total, but it's also allowed him to become the youngest player ever to reach 400 career home runs. He has good running speed and is capable of cutting his swing down to make consistent contact, but he serves his team best by hitting the ball for distance and changing the scoreboard in a hurry.

These two hitters are perennial all-stars. Both are valuable offensive players for their team. But if one tried to swing the bat like the other, he would diminish his effectiveness. Instead, both understand their strengths and capabilities and have worked to master them. You should do the same.

Too Heavy to Control

Many younger players use a bat that is too heavy, especially one that has too much weight in the barrel. When a bat is too heavy, the hands cannot control the barrel. As a result, the weight of the barrel drops the hands below the hitting plane in the downswing. When the player tries to adjust—that is, get the bat on plane—he moves upward, passing through the plane on which the pitch is traveling, and misses the ball. The swing is not only an uppercut, but also a late uppercut. The bat passes into the plane of the incoming pitch after the ball has sped past the bat into the catcher's mitt.

T-ball can promote uppercutting because the player realizes that his or her best chance at hitting a stationary ball for distance (and carry) is to drop the

Left: Swinging up at the ball will produce pop flies and topped ground balls. *Right:* Swinging level will produce line drives and gap power.

> "I think uppercut swings occur mostly because of the top hand. You're probably not using it enough. The top hand needs to work to keep the barrel above the ball. Line drives come from swinging down to the ball and through it, not up at it."
> — *Doug Glanville*

hands and uppercut, thus creating a fly-ball arc. So watch out—you may become a dynamite hitter in T-ball and a dud in baseball.

Another cause is hitching, that is, dropping the hands while in the stance below the launch position (which is just above and behind the rear shoulder) and starting the swing from this lowered position. Hitching (see page 61) causes you not only to swing too severely from low to high but also to be late in getting the barrel squared at impact.

One solution to the problem of using a heavy bat is to choke up. This brings the bat under control and should result in better manipulation of the barrel throughout the swing. Hence, you achieve a more level swing.

DRILL

■ Using a batting tee, place the ball in the center of the plate at the following heights: (1) letter high, (2) midway between letters and belt, and (3) belt high. At each position, hit ten line drives straight through the pitcher's box,

Left: Pat Burrell drops his back shoulder as he tries to do too much with this pitch. *Right:* Place a glove on the ground out in front of home plate. Try to hit the glove with each hit.

balls that would carry into centerfield for line drive singles. Choke up on the bat. On the downswing move the knob of the bat to the level of the pitch just as your hands move past your rear hip and continue forward of your midsection. Keep your hands in the palm down, palm up position as long as possible, at least until you strike the ball. Continue this drill until you can hit ten consecutive line drives at each position.

Here is special consideration for parents and coaches. When pitching to younger players, age nine or under, lower yourself—get down on one knee—so that your pitch trajectory will not be too steep. If you don't, the batters—in an effort to get the bat on plane and meet the ball squarely—will swing from low to high. This can start a bad habit—the severe uppercut swing.

Fault #29 Chopping at the Ball

Chopping at the ball means your swing path travels through the hitting zone at a downward angle, never leveling off. This type of swing makes it difficult to make square contact and initiates a steady diet of mishits—mostly ground balls. It is a fault that more often afflicts beginners.

Because the incoming pitch approaches home plate at a slight downward angle, a chopping swing allows you very little margin for error. If you clip the bottom of the baseball, you will hit a pop-up or foul ball. If you hit the top of the baseball you'll beat the ball down into the ground. Both are poor results.

"The first movement is to start down at the ball. But as you move the barrel to the hitting zone, the swing path should level off and then move slightly up. You start down, but you don't continue down through the ball."
— *Hal McRae*

Overcorrecting a Previous Fault

One cause for a chopping swing is overcompensation for an uppercut. At some point, you may have fallen into the bad habit of swinging up at the ball (as many hitters do) in an attempt to lift long, towering drives. By trying to eliminate that problem, you have overcorrected the mistake. Your goal is to have the bat level through the hitting zone so you create the largest possible hitting surface for the longest possible time as the ball approaches the point of contact.

Another root of this swing fault can stem from coaches urging their hitters to "swing down on the ball." A more accurate instruction would be, "Start down to the ball." After striding and moving the hands back to the launch position, the hands should travel forward and slightly downward. Your lead

Left: Chopping at the ball creates problems similar to uppercutting. With that swing path, it is difficult to hit the ball square. *Center:* Notice the angle of the shoulders point downward. This finish will produce hits that are beaten into the ground or cut straight up in the air. *Right:* Always remember, the forward swing starts down, but then levels off through the hitting zone.

arm (or bottom hand) pulls the bat down to the ball. Your top hand then becomes more active and begins to fire the barrel. All of this is performed without dropping the rear shoulder.

As the swing progesses and your hips rotate, your swing should gradually level off. After the barrel passes by your rear shoulder on its path to the pitch, your hands should flatten the bat out as it enters the hitting zone. Your hands and forearms keep the barrel on a level path straight through contact. After you've hit through the ball, your hands then break up into your follow-through.

Remember, start down and then level off the swing through the hitting zone. Having the fat part of the bat on a level collision course with the fat part of the ball can give opposing pitchers whiplash.

DRILL 1

■ Set up two batting tees so that one ball sits 2 to 3 inches directly behind the other. Both balls should sit at the same height. Take your stance as if you're setting up to hit the ball that is closer to the catcher. Take your normal swing and hit through both the first and second balls. In order to successfully accomplish this, your swing must stay on a level path through the hitting zone.

DRILL 2

■ In a batting cage, set up a tee on top of home plate. Aim to hit the ball back through the middle. The goal is to hit the ball on a line into the back

The object of this drill is to hit line drives into the back of the cage. To do so, you must level off your swing path through the hitting zone and hit through the ball.

net of the cage. Make contact with the ball just below its center point, and keep your top and bottom hands in the palm up, palm down position all the way through contact. If your ball travels directly down to the ground (about 15 to 20 feet in front of home plate), your swing is traveling on a downward plane as it contacts the ball. Level it off to achieve line drives.

Fault #30 Casting Your Hands

Picture a fisherman holding his rod parallel to the ground, preparing to cast his line. His hands are held in the palm up, palm down position. As he takes the rod back in a lateral motion, he extends his arms outward away from the body. He then slings the baited hook forward in a motion that is dominated by his top hand.

A phrase frequently used by batting coaches, "casting your hands," originates from this sequence. And though a fisherman may catch his dinner using this technique, a hitter will have trouble catching anything on the sweet spot of his bat.

Casting the hands is a swing fault that occurs when the hitter's hands leave the launch position. It is the first movement the hands make as they begin their path to the ball. It's also referred to as "hitting around the ball" or "getting your hands outside the ball." If your hands start to the ball by moving out and away from your body, you're casting your hands. Your hands cast out because the lead arm extends outward instead of tugging the knob of the bat toward the pitch.

No Quickness and No Knockout Punch

This particular swing fault creates two problems. The first is that it lengthens your swing. Any movement with your hands that takes the bat on a longer path to the hitting zone will make you a less effective hitter. Negative results will arise in bunches. Instead of stinging a good fastball, you'll foul it back or miss it. Pitches you drive for power will turn into weak fly balls to the opposite field. Inside strikes you remember turning on will produce balls off the fists or topped ground balls to the infield. Off-speed pitches will suddenly fool you with frequency because you have to start your hands sooner.

The second problem caused by casting your hands is a swing that will lose force. A rule of thumb: *Any movement that takes your power source out away from your body is lost energy.* Try this experiment to understand the point being made. Imagine you are a boxer. Plant your feet in an athletic position, shoulders square to the target. Cock your hand straight back behind your ear (right

Left: Notice that the hitter's hands have gotten out away from this body. This is called "casting" and it elongates your swing. *Right:* Keeping the hands closer to your body increases the strength, quickness, and control of your swing.

hand if you're a right-handed hitter and vice versa). Now fire a forehand punch at your target. It produces a quick, forceful punch.

Repeat the same exercise, but with a minor variation. Just before firing your forehand, push your fist out slightly before firing. Not only does this produce a weaker punch, but it will take longer to get to the target.

Forward and Downward

To develop an efficient swing, your first movement with your hands must be a forward movement that is slightly downward. If you could see a perfect swing in slow motion, you would notice the knob of the bat pointed at the incoming pitch for a split second.

The shortest distance between two points is a straight line. Think of your barrel as point A and the ball as point B. Fire the barrel directly to the ball. Any wasted movement will result in a wasted opportunity at the plate.

If drills fail to eliminate casting the bat, adjust your mental approach. Think about keeping your hands inside the ball as it travels toward you. As

In this soft-toss drill, the hands are in good position to the fire the barrel to the ball.

"I think one of the reasons McGwire is one of the most consistent power hitters in history is because he's so short and direct to the ball. If he were to take a big, long swing, he wouldn't hit balls out with such frequency. The fact that he's so short to the ball reduces his margin of error, and with his strength, he simply crushes pitches."

— *Charles Johnson*

the pitch is released, stay inside the ball, that is, keep your hands between your body and where you see the ball. Then fire the barrel through the hitting zone. This will keep your hands from casting out away from you.

DRILL 1

■ For this drill, use the side net of a batting cage. Place a home plate along the inside (or outside) of the net. There should be approximately 2 to 4 inches of room between the edge of home plate and the net. Assuming a pitch is coming down the middle, take a healthy cut. Your goal is to take swings without touching the net. If the end of your bat hits the net, you casting your hands out and your swing is too long. Keep practicing until you take twenty swings without hitting the net.

DRILL 2

■ For this drill, all you need is a batting tee and a net. Take your stance and position the tee to model a pitch down the middle. A player who casts his

Left: To eliminate casting, practice taking dry swings alongside a net. Place a home plate just a few inches from the inside of the net. Take swings as if the pitch were down the middle. *Center:* If you're casting your hands, the bat will hit the net. *Right:* The hitter takes a direct swing and misses the net.

hands will make contact with the outside (far side) of the ball. Right-handed hitters will hit the net off-center to the left and left-handed hitters off-center to the right. Stay on a direct path to the ball and hit it straight through the middle. To give yourself a visual image, picture a ball directly behind the ball sitting on the tee. Your goal is to hit both balls into the center of the net.

Fault #31 **The Inside-Out Swing**

The quickest and most powerful swings occur when the hands work in tandem—the bottom hand pulling the bat and the top hand firing the barrel through the ball. This is not the case if you're using what is called an "inside-out" swing.

The inside-out swing means the lead arm is dominating your stroke. The barrel is dragged through the strike zone, an action created by the lead arm straightening more slowly and the wrist of the top hand holding its cocked position longer, and then only partially uncocking upon contact. Instead of aggressively slamming the ball to the outfield gaps, you weakly serve the ball to the opposite field.

Identifying an inside-out swing is simple. For starters, the barrel trails the hands at contact. Instead of the hands being square to the ball or behind it at contact, they will be ahead of the ball. Because of this, hits will travel to the opposite field, slicing or tailing when hit in the air and robbing you of distance.

Locating the Fault's Origin

A number of factors contribute to an inside-out swing. The first place to look is at your hands in the pre-swing. Are your hands tucked in very close to your body in your stance? From this position, you may have minimal separation (see page 58) and simply push your hands to the ball. Your lead arm moves out to the ball, instead of moving down and forward to the correct point of contact. The top hand follows along with the bottom hand, then rolls over after contact.

Hitters also develop an inside-out swing because they're late starting to the ball. In other words, they get "handcuffed." If this happens, check the position of your hands and distance of your separation. If you're loading your hands too far back, you may not be giving yourself enough time to get to the ball. A simple—but wrong—adjustment is to pull your hands in and push the bat to the ball. This adjustment may help you make contact, but the swing lacks the force and bat speed to hit the ball with authority.

Poor timing of your separation—hands away from body—can make you late as well. If you're taking your stride and separating your hands after the ball is released, you won't have the time to generate a powerful swing. Once again, you'll compensate by pulling your arms, hitting the ball too deep in the hitting zone.

Last, if your mental approach is conservative rather than aggressive, your swing will be adversely affected. Making contact is an objective at the plate, but not to the point where you sacrifice power. The more tentative you are at bat, the longer you'll wait to commit to swinging. The deeper the ball gets in the hitting zone, the greater the chance you'll resort to an inside-out swing. Seeing the ball long is good, but not so long that you don't have enough time to get the barrel square to the ball.

Poor Results

Though you may make consistent contact with an inside-out swing, the results will be disappointing. You'll generate very little power. Because inside-out swingers let the ball travel too deep into the strike zone, their hips are unable to fully rotate. Catching up to good fastballs will be difficult. Your bat speed will accelerate only after contact, because the top hand is finally able to contribute to your wrist snap. A slow bat with no pop is a poor trade for ensuring contact.

"Well I think an inside-out swing can be a good two-strike approach, but using it all the time will be detrimental. You lose pop or power and the ability to drive the ball. Once pitchers notice you "inside-out" the ball, they'll pound you inside all day."
— *Dave Gallagher, college coach and professional hitting instructor*

Left: The lead arm dominates an inside-out swing. It pushes the handle of the bat to the ball as the barrel trails behind. *Right:* A good swing allows the top hand to fire the barrel so it's even with the hands at the point of contact.

You'll hit a lot of balls into the air with an inside-out swing. The top hand is practically dormant throughout the swing. Since the top hand is integral to keeping the barrel above the ball, the bat will often dip as it enters the hitting zone. When the barrel drops below the ball, fly balls follow.

You must first find the root of the fault before making an adjustment. Is it your hand positioning? Do you wait too long to get started? Is your approach too passive? Ask your coach to observe your swing, or better yet, videotape your at bats and see for yourself what you're doing wrong.

Move Hands to a Stronger Position

Make sure your hands aren't too close to your body. If they are, free them up by moving them just in front of your back shoulder, approximately 5 or 6 inches away from your body. Just before the pitcher releases the ball, move them straight back to the launch position (shoulder height just to rear of your shoulder). From that point, fire the barrel directly to the ball.

Visual imagery may help you understand what the proper hand action should feel like. Imagine chopping down a tree with an axe. To really dig the axe into the tree, you've got to fire the blade using the wrist snap of both hands. The top hand actively participates in firing the blade. Pushing the blade into the tree with a stroke dominated by your lead arm wouldn't feel powerful, would it?

Attack the Ball

A passive approach is easy to overcome. Simply go on the attack. Explode on the ball when you see a good pitch. Picture Mike Piazza, Jeff Bagwell, Ken Griffey Jr., or Vladimir Guerrero. They certainly don't get cheated when they swing the bat. They see the ball as long as possible and then unleash violent hacks at the ball. As long as you maintain balance and keep your body and hands tension-free, take your rips.

DRILL 1

■ Grab the bat with your top hand, holding it just above the handle (one-third of the way up the bat). With a coach or teammate soft-tossing, fire the barrel directly to the ball with your top hand. Use only your wrist and

This drill isolates the top hand and its role in the swing. Choke up and feel your wrist and forearm fire the barrel straight to the ball. Your shoulder should not influence your swing.

Times to Use the Inside-Out Swing

The inside-out swing limits your hitting potential, but there are times when it may be useful for right-handed hitters. For example, when trying to advance a runner from second to third base, the inside-out swing may be the best method of directing the ball.

With nobody out and a runner on second base, you should make an attempt to move the runner over to third (unless otherwise instructed by your coach). Good pitchers know this, and they will throw inside to make your job difficult. Simply allow the ball to get deep, pull your hands in toward your body, and push the ball to the right side of second base. You've accomplished your job and even have a chance of slipping the ball through the hole.

forearm to swing the bat. Your rear shoulder should not factor into the swing. Concentrate on being short and quick to the ball, keeping the barrel above the ball until contact.

DRILL 2

■ Place a batting tee 10 feet in front of home plate. Set your stance to the tee as if you're hitting a pitch down the middle. Try to hit line drives into the back net of the cage. Adjust your swing according to your results. For example, hitting a ball into the pull-side of the net means you're using too much top hand. Feel the bottom hand stay through the ball a bit longer on your next swing.

DRILL 3

■ Have a coach or teammate toss you short batting practice (15 to 20 feet) from behind an "L-screen." Work on pitches thrown to the inside corner. Open your hips and fire the barrel out in front of home plate to meet the ball. Keep both hands through the ball at contact, driving the ball to your pull side.

Fault #32 Dropping the Barrel on Low Strikes

To pitchers, the low strike is the most desired, most sought after pitch. It induces more playable hits, such as ground balls, than other strikes. Pitching coaches constantly remind their hurlers, "Keep the ball down." If you want to become a good hitter, you must learn to handle low strikes.

Left: Dropping the barrel to the ball decreases your chance of square contact. *Right:* Use your legs to lower your body and head to the ball. This allows you to put your swing on a level plane with the pitch.

Don't Drop the Barrel

"I recommend a short, level swing and [hitting] the ball back through the middle with minimal head movement. This will bring the most consistent success."

— Alex Rodriguez

Too many hitters mistakenly drop their bat (and barrel) to the ball on low strikes. Instead of lowering their legs to get the bat on a level plane with the incoming pitch, hitters get lazy. They simply "drop the barrel."

Dropping the barrel makes square contact difficult. To understand this, hold your bat vertical with the knob pointing to the sky. Notice that the barrel is only one baseball wide. If your barrel approached the ball at this exaggerated angle (perpendicular to the ground), your hitting surface would have practically no margin of error. To achieve square contact would take incredible hand-to-eye coordination. As you angle the bat upward (raise the barrel away from you), you begin to broaden the hitting surface. When the bat is perfectly level, the barrel of the bat above the label is approximately four baseballs wide. (The sweet spot of the barrel provides the best results.) This gives you the greatest chance of hitting the ball hard.

Low strikes can be hit with authority, but it's difficult to accomplish when dropping the barrel. Many times you'll swing through pitches simply because your hitting surface is so narrow. If you swing a split-second early, the end of

He can do more than just pitch. Greg Maddux goes down to get this one.

the bat will dip under and come up at the ball, producing many high pops and fly balls (also known as "easy outs"). If it's a little late, the bat will strike down on the ball and smother it into the ground (also known as an "easy ground ball").

On the rare occasions you hit the ball off the sweet spot, the angle of your swing path may cause your hits to slice or hook. Any side spin deducts from the distance your hit would have traveled if contacted squarely.

Getting the Bat on a Flat Plane

The swing is just the end result of your fault. The actual mistake occurs earlier. The mistake is made when you decide to use exclusively your hands (instead of your legs) to attack the low strike. This is the wrong decision. Use your legs to lower your body and swing the bat on a level plane. By lowering your legs, you'll lower your hands and eyes closer to the pitch. This allows you to produce a level swing at the ball. When you see a pitch down, think legs.

To lower your body, "sit down," that is, allow greater flex in your legs. This occurs after the stride foot has planted and you begin your rotation. Your balance remains intact because you're simply lowering your center of gravity.

Left: React to low pitches tossed underhand. Make sure the feeder moves back behind the screen after tossing. *Right:* From a 45-degree angle, work specifically on hitting low strikes. Focus on getting your bat on plane with the ball.

Another advantage to lowering your body is getting your eyes closer to the ball. This improves hand-to-eye coordination and increases your chances of contact. Remember, a marksman holds his rifle up near his eye, not down by his hip.

DRILL 1

■ Have a partner toss underhand pitches to you from 15 feet. (Your coach or teammate should stand behind the straight edge of a "L-screen.") Have him toss each pitch down in the strike zone so you can work on lowering your body to the ball. After approximately fifteen swings, request pitches of varying heights. React and adjust to the different locations.

Note: Do not practice lowering your body until after your stride foot has planted. In game situations, you will not recognize the pitch as a low strike until your stride foot is down and the ball has left the pitcher's hand.

DRILL 2

■ Take soft-toss swings at balls delivered at a 45-degree angle. Have your partner toss balls up in the strike zone, or down in the strike zone. As he releases each ball, he should yell, "Up" or "Down." Use your legs to lower your body when hitting "low" tosses, and raise your hands to get on a level plane with the ball when hitting "up" tosses.

Fault #33 Swinging Up at High Strikes

The fault of swinging up at high strikes stems from dropping the hands too soon or too far down from the launch position. Even when your hands start in the proper launch position, they can be lowered on the approach to the ball without much conscious intent on your part in at least two ways. For one, the stride naturally widens your base, which slightly lowers your entire body, including the hands. Add to that the possibility that you drop them as a matter of individual batting style. It's the latter that can cause so much trouble.

The launch position is not the first position of your hands when you step into the batter's box. However, *it is the last position before you move directly to the ball.* Thus, when you take your stance you should start with your hands as close as possible to the launch position. This will allow you to get into position without a lot of movement. If you have to drop, raise, or pull your hands in from a great distance, it can throw off your timing.

The distance that you lower the hands from the launch position depends on the height of the ball in the strike zone. The improper approach to a pitch high in the strike zone is taken when a batter drops or drifts his hands down too low from the launch position—that is, he allows the hands to move to a position from which the only path to the ball is a severe uppercut.

The results of this fault are as predictable as night following day: lots of missed swings and two varieties of mishits: (1) pop-ups when intercepting the ball slightly below its equator and (2) topped ground balls when striking the top half of the ball.

Get the Hands on Plane

The proper technique for hitting a pitch in the top half of the strike zone is to move the hands on their approach to the same height as the pitch. Get and keep the barrel of the bat on a level plane that will keep it in a long path of interception with the ball. You want to either "get on top of the ball," that is,

> "Pitchers are always taught to work down in the strike zone. It's much more difficult for a hitter to make square contact with a low strike. A lot of times they'll just drop the barrel and give you an easy out."
>
> — *Jesse Orosco*

Left: Tony Eusebio swings up at this high pitch. His only hope is that the ball carries foul. *Right:* Raise your hands to get the bat on plane with the pitch. This will help to produce line drives to the outfield, rather than pop flies to the infield.

"I'm a high ball hitter. The key to hitting the high strike is keeping your hands on top of the ball. You can't swing up at a high strike. That's upper-cutting and all you'll hit is fly balls. I get my hands on top of the ball, and swing the bat level through the zone."
— *Doug Glanville*

meet it on the top side of its equator, or meet it squarely at the equator. The latter will produce a line drive, and the former point of contact will create either a top-spin line drive or a fast-moving, top-spin ground ball.

If for any reason you hit the ball below the equator—contact that propels the ball at more than a 45-degree angle off the bat—you'll be an easy out. This produces lazy fly balls and pop-ups. Balls leaving the bat at 45 degrees, however, have the potential to carry over the fence.

DRILL

■ Here is a soft-toss drill that helps you ingrain recognition of high strikes and a disciplined approach to hitting them. A partner or coach alerts you to location of the tosses by calling out "Up" when tossing a high strike and "Down" when tossing a low strike. As batter, you make split-second adjustments upon hearing the calls. You keep your hands up for high strikes and take a path to the ball that meets the ball squarely or slightly above its

Tony Gwynn does an exceptional job of getting his hands on top of the ball. The key to doing this is shown in the top right photo. After recognizing the height of the pitch, Gwynn keeps his hands up as he moves from the launch position. He never allows them to move down. He then rotates his hips and fires the bat on a level path.

During soft-toss drills, work specifically on high strikes and focus on getting your bat on plane with the ball.

equator. For the low strikes, you slightly lower your legs, and thus your entire body, and bring the bat on a plane that contacts the ball at its equator (result: line drive).

Your partner repeats tosses without alerting you to position in strike zone. You make adjustment and after swinging tell tosser how you judged the pitch, "Up" or "Down." Tosser gives instant feedback and critique, informing your if your call was correct and if your adjustment was good.

Fault #34 Failing to Snap Wrists

You cannot have a good swing without properly snapping the wrists. The snapping of the wrists fires the barrel of the bat into the path of the incoming pitch. The failure to snap your wrists leads to a major power outage—weak, flaring fly balls and slow-moving groundouts.

Wrist Snap—The Action That Gives You Pop in Your Swing

Here's how to spot a swing without a wrist snap. For right-handers, the left side dominates the swing. The right hand and right arm are nearly dormant;

they passively hold the bat but do not manipulate it. The left side of the body and left arm pull the arms through the hitting zone in a long sweeping arc.

This type of approach to the ball leaves much of the strike zone unreachable. You simply cannot pull the head of the bat into the ball's path as fast as you can propel it with the right hand pushing and the wrists snapping.

It also makes it nearly impossible to keep the head and body from moving laterally—too far forward—when swinging. Because the left side of the body must square the bat without the aid of the wrists, it moves ahead of the impact point. Result? A sweeping, slow swing with no pop at impact!

Without the proper wrist snap you'll be consistently late when swinging at fast balls, have trouble handling inside pitches, and be regularly fooled on off-speed pitches because of the need to start your swing too early.

Cock the Wrist and Fire

To make the proper wrist snap you must first assume the proper wrist set. Pretend to make a pistol out of your left hand with your index finger as the barrel and your thumb up in the air as if it were a hammer. Pull directly back

> "Wrist snap is one of the key elements to the swing. If you do it correctly, it keeps the barrel through the hitting zone without changing its path or without lifting it over the ball and creating top-spin. It's not a wrist roll, it should be a wrist snap."
>
> — *Dave Gallagher*

Left: When a hitter fails to snap his wrists, the bat decelerates through the hitting zone. The finish will appear as if he's cut his swing short. *Right:* Snapping the wrists accelerates your bat to and through the ball and finishes in full follow-through.

Notice the difference in the position of Paul O'Neill's top hand in the two photos. *Left:* His bat is on path with the pitch; his top hand has yet to fire. *Right:* His top hand has propelled the bat to and through the ball. That wrist snap helped send this pitch to right-center field for a triple.

on your thumb (the hammer) in the direction of your forearm and cock your wrist. That's the proper wrist set. This is how to hold the wrists when grasping the bat in the launch position.

Setting the wrist properly is important because it creates the leverage needed to propel the barrel of the bat. This leverage is created when the wrists snap.

What is the correct action in snapping the wrists? For starters, take a direct path to the ball from the launch position with your hands leading the swing. Your goal is to bring the barrel on the most direct path for intercepting the ball. As you bring the bat down from the launch position and forward, position the hands so that the top hand is facing palm up and the bottom hand is facing palm down. At this point in the swing, the barrel of the bat trails behind the hands—nearly 90 degrees—until the hands pass your front side, which has rotated open (belt buckle now facing the pitcher).

Then, as you move your hands the final 6 to 8 inches toward contact, the wrists snap the bat through the hitting zone. This is a powerful move, the unhinging of the wrists and propelling of the bat's head into the path of the pitch. This snap fires the barrel of the bat, giving you pop when you hit the ball.

Be careful not to roll the top hand over the bottom hand too soon. This also helps propel the barrel of the bat but places the hands in a weaker position when done before or at impact. Rolling the top hand too soon is a devastating fault. As a player improves his overall bat speed, so will he improve the speed with which he rolls the barrel out of the hitting zone. This will make the player more vulnerable to off-speed pitches and fastballs away in the strike zone. And as the player moves to higher levels of play, he will face pitchers who have higher velocity and can consistently throw to these spots of vulnerability.

DRILLS

■ These drills will help you develop the proper technique and reinforce the feeling of smacking the ball with an explosive wrist snap, rather than just passively placing the bat in the ball's path.

1. Lay a bat in front of you, perpendicular to an imaginary line between your feet. Place the handle between your feet in the middle. Grasp the bat and pick it up, bat and arms extended in front. Then move the bat slightly to the right. Pull the head or barrel up and toward you by hinging or setting your wrists. Move the bat to the rear of your right shoulder. You are now in the launch position with the proper setting of the wrists. Practice this until you can do it without thinking.

2. Next, place a ball on a tee and place the ball opposite your stride foot. Approach the ball with your bat by slowly extending your arms and hands into the palm up, palm down position. Fold the right elbow down and in to the right side and then extend it as you move the bat to the point of contact. Unhinge the wrists and knock the ball from the tee. Repeat ten times. Continue drill for several sessions, adding more speed each time when approaching the ball.

3. Have a partner hold the barrel of your bat with both hands while you are in the contact position and your wrists are still cocked. Then unhinge the wrists against your partner's resistance. Next, hold your bat at the contact point with the top hand palm facing the pitcher and the bottom hand palm facing the catcher as if they had begun to roll prematurely. Now try to advance the barrel against his resistance. You can immediately feel the inferior strength of the latter position. The desired hand position at and through contact is the first position—palm up, palm down, wrists horizontally hinged.

Take a healthy cut at a ball on the tee and drive it to the outfield. Make sure you finish your swing with a complete follow-through.

Fault #35 Dragging the Bat Through the Hitting Zone

Here is a fault that appears at two distinct levels, beginners and advanced hitters. At both levels, the fault is the same—the bat is not accelerating properly through the hitting zone—but the telltale signs and body actions are very different.

Slow Hips, Slow Hands = Slow Swing

At the beginner's level, this fault is the result of a player simultaneously rotating the hips, shifting weight from the rear leg to the front leg, pulling and pushing the bat through the hitting zone. The swing looks more like a glide with the entire body swaying back to front. Usually, a beginner with this fault will also rise up slightly on the front leg as he finishes the swing, much like a golfer who finishes with a very vertical posture, weight set on the forward leg. With this swing there is no follow-through—the bat stops just beyond contact.

Players exhibiting this fault are overly concerned with making contact with the ball. They often do, but do not hit the ball very far because the swing delivers no appreciable force when striking the ball.

"Anyone who thinks long swings produce long hits is preaching inaccurate information. It's absolutely inaccurate. Be short and explode through the ball. A short swing means quickness and you've got to be quick in this game."

— Mark McGwire

To correct this swing, the player needs literally to begin to learn and apply the correct swing techniques from the ground up. Here are the most critical corrections:

1. Feet—the ball and toes of the rear foot should pivot
2. Rotation—the hips and torso should coil and uncoil, belly button facing the pitcher
3. Weight transfer—keep shoulders level when moving weight onto front leg/foot
4. Hands—top hand snaps the barrel toward ball, front arm pulls

Here are the components of a good swing. Reviewing them is a good start in correcting the fault of dragging the bat through the hitting zone:

1. Recoil—Go back to go forward. The recoil can be as minimal as a slight inward turn of the knee or as exaggerated as a front leg kick.
2. Step—As the pitcher is releasing the ball, take a short, soft step toward him.

There are a variety of reasons a hitter's barrel drags through the zone: tension, overswinging, pulling the front shoulder out early, premature hip rotation, barring the lead arm, swinging a bat that's too heavy. The key is to detect where the problem lies and make the adjustment.

Stay relaxed and feel your hands and wrists snap the barrel to the ball.

3. Separate—As the pitch is released, the hands and the front foot should separate. The hands should move to the back while the lead foot steps out. This is called the "launch position."
4. Vision—Pick up the velocity, location, and type of pitch so you can time your swing correctly.
5. Adjust—Once you've determined the type of pitch, you need to move your hands and your body accordingly.
6. Contact—Bring the barrel of the bat to the ball. On an inside pitch, this would be out in front of the plate; for one over the middle of the plate, it would be at the front portion of the plate; and for an outside pitch, contact would be at the middle to back part of the plate.
7. Palm Up, Palm Down—As you make contact, your top hand should face up toward the sky and your bottom hand down to the ground. This is called the "palm-up, palm-down position."
8. Roll Over—After you have hit through the ball, roll your wrists over.
9. Follow Through—Finish your swing. Young hitters are often guilty of cutting down their swings.
10. Head Down—Keep your head down on the entire swing. This will help keep your front side closed until you rotate and uncoil the torso.

When the barrel drags, the hitter frequently gets jammed (hits the ball below the barrel of the bat).

Front Side Opens Too Soon

When the advanced player exhibits a dragging of the bat through the strike zone, his flaw is often rooted in a premature opening of the front side (hips and shoulders). Any action that allows the front side to open too soon upsets the rhythm of the swing and causes it to lose speed. When the front side opens prematurely, the hands are carried forward slightly, thus robbing them of a full arc of acceleration. Thus, when the bat moves slowly or decelerates through the hitting zone, power is lost. The result: weak ground balls or pop-ups, often to the opposite field.

In a correct swing, the hands and the hips work together upon planting of the front foot. The hips rotate quickly, the torso uncoils, and the hands propel the barrel of the bat toward the ball. The sequence of action—turning of the front hip, pulling of the lead arm, pushing by the top hand, and uncocking of the wrists from a shoulder-high, wrapped position to palms up, palms down at contact—speeds up the barrel of the bat, much as the cracking of a whip accelerates the tip. There is no time to hesitate once the body moves to swing.

Two factors, more than any others, enable the swing to pick up speed through and past the point of impact: the rotating hips and flying hands (firing the bat toward the ball).

Playing pepper teaches the hitter to put the barrel on the ball using his hands and wrists. Players who practice pepper with regularity develop a knack for finding the ball with the barrel.

DRILL

■ Pepper is a great drill to work on bringing the barrel directly to the ball. A relaxed effort will eliminate additional movements like casting. Grab a few players and practice hitting the ball off the sweet spot of the bat with a short, efficient swing.

Fault #36 Cutting Your Swing Short (Limited or No Extension)

A major league baseball scout once summarized what it was that would prompt him to take a closer look at a pitching prospect: "I look for arm action that is short in the back and long in the front." The same is true for batters. A short, compact swing with a full follow-through gets results—and draws the attention of scouts. The phrase "short in the back" refers to an efficient move to the batter's launch position. It shows early preparation and enables the batter to take a short, direct path to the ball. "Long in the front" indicates that the batter has moved his arms to nearly full or full extension. This provides the fastest and most powerful delivery of the bat barrel to impact and through the hitting zone.

The action or movement after contact with the ball is important. You must keep the arms moving toward full extension. Any swing that cuts short the arc of the arm swing is seriously flawed.

You may be cutting your swing short if you find that you are repeatedly

1. Hitting ground balls to the pull side of the field
2. Pulling balls, grounders and fly balls, into foul territory
3. Hitting balls weakly, with no pop
4. Failing to hit balls that are over the middle and outside of the plate
5. Hitting top-spin line drives or hooking line drives toward the foul line

These results are symptomatic of a shortened follow-through, because the arms are working improperly when moving to and through the hitting area. A shortened swing occurs when the top-hand arm folds over the bottom-hand arm too soon. This causes the bottom-hand arm to fold at the elbow. Thus, the length of the arc—the distance from the shoulder to the hands on the bat—is shortened. The shortened arc slows the speed of the bat and takes it prematurely off the plane it must travel to meet the pitch.

"You want to be as short to the ball as possible with a long extension through the baseball. Keeping your bat moving through the ball after contact is what helps to get your entire body into hitting the ball."

— *Mark McGwire*

Left: Young hitters are notorious for stopping their swing immediately after contact. To stop so quickly, the hitter has to decelerate his swing before making contact. This will reduce the speed and distance of your hits. *Right:* Finish your swing behind your back shoulder.

Full Extension at or Just Beyond Contact

In a proper baseball swing, the bottom-hand arm starts slightly bent at the elbow in the stance and launch position. It first moves downward and forward and then begins to straighten as the bat moves from the launch position to impact. It reaches full extension either just beyond impact or at impact, but rarely before impact unless you are fooled by an off-speed pitch and strike the ball well out in front. The top-hand arm also straightens incrementally throughout the swing and reaches full extension—also forming a triangle with the shoulders—at impact or slightly beyond impact. If both arms are fully extended before impact, you've been fooled with an off-speed pitch or you're bedeviled with another fault.

Remember that the top hand supplies more power and direction than the bottom hand when propelling the barrel of the bat to the ball. This is because the top hand is closer to the barrel and the uncocking of the top-hand wrist fires the barrel of the bat to the ball. The bottom hand helps to guide the bat toward the ball, but the top hand supplies the thunder.

DRILLS

■ Allowing your top hand to dominate your swing often results in a swing that is too short. The top hand rolls the head of the bat over—and out of the swing plane or path needed to meet the ball squarely. There are several drills to promote better coordination of the hands and arms through impact. Here are a couple.

1. Set a ball on a batting tee. Grip the bat with the bottom hand only, choking up 6 to 8 inches. Extend your arm so that the bat is perpendicular to an imaginary line from the pitcher's mound to the plate. Your palm is facing down. Draw the bat back to your launch position, keeping only one hand on the handle. Next, deliver a short, direct blow to the back of the ball. Try to drive it straight toward the imaginary pitcher. Continue the movement of your arm until it is fully extended. Repeat twenty-five times.

   Regrip the bat handle with both hands and place the bat just behind the ball, parallel to the ground, the hands in the palm up, palm down position. Repeat the remainder of the drill as described above for twenty-five repetitions, trying to drive the ball to the back of the batting cage.

   After several sessions with the tee, repeat the drill using soft toss.

2. With a partner providing soft tosses, take normal swings but stop moving your hands forward upon contact. Do not roll or snap your wrists—keep

To hit the ball with authority to the outfield, you've got to be short to it, and long through it.

them in the palm up, palm down position. This allows you to feel the position your hands should be in at contact. Repeat twenty-five times.

Fault #37 Releasing the Top Hand Too Soon

The late Charley Lau, major league hitting coach and author of *The Art of Hitting .300*, a classic book on batting, once visited Australia to teach hitting. Upon his arrival and first observations of the styles of the Australian batters, he discovered that his teachings had arrived before he did. The Australians had already begun modeling their swings by following the 10 Absolutes of Hitting presented in his book. However, they had misinterpreted his final absolute that called for *hitting through the ball*. Lau's instruction was to keep both hands on the bat until (1) the momentum of the follow-through and (2) the extension of the top hand and arm were completed, which came as the bat moved around toward the back of the body at the finish of the swing.

However, the Aussies were releasing the top hand too soon and the results

Left: For those who release the top hand in their follow through, here is an example of releasing too soon. *Right:* If you choose to release the top hand, it occurs well after contact. Notice the top hand traveled to the rear shoulder before releasing.

were calamitous. They were producing weakly struck balls with little or no pop at contact. Lau quickly set about to correct the problem. He showed them when to release the top hand and how to employ it throughout the swing, on approach, at contact, and during the follow-through. What follows is a good summary of the proper two-hand technique.

The top hand is the hand that fires the head or barrel of the bat into the path of the incoming pitch. It complements the other arm and hand, which are pulling—not pushing—the bat through the hitting zone, led by the uncoiling of the hips and torso.

Top Hand Supplies the Power

The top hand, however, is the dominant hand in supplying the power. It must remain on the handle throughout the forward swing. It unhinges during the initial stage, when the bat leaves its vertical position and travels horizontally along the swing plane. Then it turns the palm up so that upon contact the hands are palm up (top hand) and palm down (bottom hand). It stays firmly on the bat's handle until the top-hand arm reaches full extension and the top-hand wrist and forearm (for a right-handed batter, the right arm,

Striking Down Your Slump

Batting slumps are inevitable. They happen to even the very best hitters in the game. But how do you get out of them? Players try everything from new bats, to new stances, to a new pair of socks. Ballplayers tend to be very superstitious, but slumps are a reality.

Just as there is no standard technique to hitting a baseball, there is no one way to cure a slump. These are some methods hitters turn to when they're struggling at the dish. Find one that works for you.

Extra batting practice—There is no substitute for hard work. All-time career hits leader Pete Rose used to take swings until his hands bled. Extra batting practice will accomplish two things. (1) It increases your repetitions, allowing you to iron out your swing. Just make sure you practice correctly. Acknowledge what you're doing wrong in the game and make the proper adjustment. (2) It will give you a psychological edge. Knowing that you've put extra time in will elevate your self-esteem and breed confidence.

Back to the basics—When things go awry, it may be time to go back to what made you a good hitter. Dust off the drills you worked on during pre-season and refine your mechanics. Take swings off the batting tee, hit soft toss in the cage, incorporate dry swings into your pre-game routine. You don't have to reinvent your swing when you're struggling. You simply may have to repair it.

Visualization—Negative thoughts bring about negative results. When things aren't going well, it's difficult to ignore negative imagery. Positive visualization exercises can help to produce better results. Think back to when things were going well. Feed off your great performances of the past. Visualize hitting a line drive up the middle, recall the three-run home run you hit a month ago, think about the great at bat you had when you fouled off four pitches before lining a base hit to the opposite field. To be a winner, you have to think like a winner.

Watch videotape—Being told what you're doing wrong at the plate is one thing, but seeing it can facilitate your path to recovery. Coaches and teammates may mention a swing flaw time and time again, but you may not believe it until you see it with your own eyes. If you're slumping badly and have access to a video camera, use it. As they say, a picture is worth a thousand words.

A fresh look—Many hitters respond to change. They feel that if they're doing something different, it discharges the bad hitter from the past and gives birth to a new, successful hitter. Subtle adjustments like raising your hands, flexing more at the knees, adding some preliminary movement, or changing your position in the batter's box may act as a vehicle to a fresh outlook.

Attitude adjustment—If you're walking up to the plate hoping to get a hit, you need to adjust your mental approach. You must believe in yourself and your ability. Every time you grab a bat, you should say, "I know I'm going to get a hit." Hoping you'll succeed indicates insecurity. Knowing you'll succeed demonstates confidence.

It's just a game—Keep in mind that baseball is a game. It's not life or death. Enjoy yourself on the field. Think back to when you were a kid and you couldn't wait to get your turn at the plate. Hitting is fun and your time to shine.

wrist, and hand) have fully rotated over the top of the bottom-hand arm and wrist. A caution: Do not rotate the top hand over the bottom hand until after contact. An early rotation raises the head of the bat and usually results in contact that produces ground balls.

When the top hand has completed its full extension and rotation its effective work is done—there's nothing left but the follow-through, which is really nothing more than the continuation of the swing after the ball has been struck.

Choose the Technique That Suits You

You can release your top hand after reaching the point of full extension or you can keep it on the bat; the latter will then cause your bottom-hand arm to fold at the elbow. Either style works, so choose the one that works for you but make sure you allow the swing to run its course. Don't cut it short at the point of contact, and don't release or loosen the grip of the top hand before contact.

Major league slugger Mo Vaughn sums up the most important point when considering top-hand action: "It's important to hit through the baseball, get good arm extension, and finish the swing. If you don't follow through, the ball won't go anywhere."

Vary Your Technique with Pitch Location

Certain pitch locations may dictate how you swing through to completion. Pitches that are away, that is, over the outside portions of the plate, or pitches that break over the outside of the plate can be better handled by a full extension of the bottom-hand arm. You can literally flick the barrel of the bat at the ball and slap the pitch into the opposite field. New York Yankee Paul O'Neill is very good at this technique. You can make this technique easier by releasing the top hand in the follow-through. This helps keep the bat on plane and propel the ball the opposite way. Your hips do not finish with your belt buckle facing the pitcher or the hitter's side of the pitcher's position on the field. Rather, your belt buckle faces to the opposite field side of the pitcher.

However, when turning on an inside pitch or hitting a strike on the inner half of the plate, it is better to keep the top hand on the bat and fully extend the top-hand arm. This gives you a tremendous power burst because—in a microsecond of synchronization—your entire left side is pulling, your hips are rotating, your torso is uncoiling, your top-hand arm is extending, and your top hand is firing the barrel of the bat into the ball. Here it's better to hold onto the bat with both hands through the entire swing.

DRILL

■ You can practice this by hitting soft-toss pitches. Have a partner toss ten pitches to the outside of the strike zone. Swing with a full extension of the

Left: Some hitters allow the location of the pitch to dictate their follow-through. Here, the pitch is middle-in so both hands stay on the bat. *Right:* Using this short-toss drill, practice keeping both hands on the bat. Focus on hitting through the ball with both hands.

bottom-hand arm and release the top hand after contact. Then swing at ten pitches over the inside of the plate. Fully rotate and keep the top hand on the bat throughout. Check your belt buckle upon completion—it should be facing to the hitter's side of the pitcher (for a right-handed batter, it should face the shortstop's position on the field).

Fault #38 Pulling Your Head Off the Ball

"You're pulling your head off the ball." This is a familiar cry from parents, coaches, and teammates. Pulling your head off the ball occurs when the head (and eyes) move with the front shoulder during the swing. The eyes stop tracking the ball on its path to the plate, and you end up trying to hit a moving object you're not looking at. It's tough to hit what you can't see.

Eyes Will Follow the Front Shoulder

Here's what to look for when you suspect you're pulling your head out. As your swing begins its path to the ball, your front shoulder rotates open (slightly), and your arms extend out over or in front of home plate. (Slowly

Left: When the head pulls off the ball, making contact becomes blind luck. *Right:* The head should face down at the point of contact. Although it's impossible to actually see the ball hit the bat, attempting to do so trains you to see the ball as long as possible.

simulate a swing and observe the movement of the front shoulder.) The head does one of two things: It remains still and locked on the flight of the pitch, or it moves *with* the front shoulder and "pulls off the ball." If the head moves with the shoulder, your eyes stop tracking the ball and lose sight of the pitch. Swing . . . and a miss!

It's frustrating when a near-perfect swing results in strike one. Watch the pitch as long as possible and you'll cut down your misses.

See the Ball as Long as Possible

Ever notice Tony Gwynn or Scott Rolen take a pitch? They watch the ball all the way into the catcher's mitt. They're tracking the ball throughout its flight, even when they don't swing. You should do the same.

"See the ball hit the bat" is a cliché coaches often use. The laws of science prove that this is impossible. High-speed photography reveals that hitters track the ball in their central field of vision until it's about 12 feet away. They see and follow the ball the final 12 feet up until contact with peripheral vision. The ball and bat travel too fast for the hitter to literally see the bat meet the ball. But coaches use this phrase for good reason. By attempting to see the ball hit the bat you train yourself to see the ball as long as possible. It gives you the greatest opportunity for consistent contact.

Whether you're suffering from a momentary lapse of concentration or trying to take an early peak at where your batted ball travels, pulling your head off the ball is a common mistake. Keep in mind that overswinging is the number one reason hitters pull their head off the ball. In fact, any strenuous physical act in sports results in the athlete pulling his head out or up. A quarterback throwing a football as far as he can, a track athlete exerting the hammer throw or shot put, or even a weightlifter picking a heavy barbell off the floor—their heads snap out or up. Stop overswinging and you'll keep your head and body under control.

DRILL 1

■ Set a ball on a hitting tee. Look out toward the pitcher's mound (or where it would be). As you stride, visualize the path of the pitch down to the ball sitting on the tee, then swing. Keep your eyes on the top of the tee until

> "After I won the batting title in 1993, I became too pull-conscious. I went up to the plate with the mindset I was going to find a pitch I could pull for power. Inevitably, this would make me pull my head off the pitch early. It's tough enough to hit good pitching, but it's nearly impossible to hit what you can't see."
>
> — *John Olerud*

When taking swings off the tee, exaggerate the amount of time you keep your eyes on the point of contact. This drill stops you from pulling your head off the ball.

well after contact is made. Exaggerate the amount of time you keep your head down until the technique becomes habit.

DRILL 2

■ During batting practice, devote an entire round to hitting the ball to the opposite field. Whether the pitch is inside, outside, high, or low, allow the ball to travel deep into the strike zone. Hitting to the opposite field forces your eyes to stay on the ball longer and keeps your head from pulling off the pitch.

Fault #39 "Feeling" for Pitches

To hit the ball hard, you must attack the ball with an assertive, confident swing. That rings true whether you're red hot at the plate or mired in a horrific slump. Struggling hitters often cut back on their swing and "feel" for pitches. This is a poor approach that will create or continue unsatisfactory results.

There are two main power sources for hitting a baseball—the power supplied by the pitcher, and the power supplied by your swing. The power supplied by the pitcher is out of your control. You cannot dictate whether he throws a 75-mph fastball or 95-mph fastball. You do, however, control how fast the barrel of the bat travels through the hitting zone to the point of contact. If your efforts are anything less than 100 percent, you are unnecessarily sacrificing power.

> "You want to be aggressive at the plate and swing the bat with authority. You certainly don't want to be 'feeling' for pitches. When you feel for a pitch, you're hoping to hit it and that illustrates a lack of confidence."
>
> — *Mike Bordick*

Avoid Deceleration

When you cut down on the speed of your swing, the bat will travel through the hitting zone for a longer period of time. True, this increases your chances of contact, but if that is your only goal, you may as well square around to bunt at every plate appearance. The number one goal is to hit the ball hard. Weakly hit balls rarely get you on first base.

Other mechanical mistakes often develop from this approach. For example, feeling for the pitch encourages front foot hitting. Because you're simply looking to "meet" the ball, the tendency is to go to the pitch. Your weight quickly transfers forward onto your stride foot, which inhibits hip rotation. The strength and speed generated from your hip torque quickly degenerates. Also, you diminish the power from your hands and wrists because they're not exploding through the ball. Instead, they gingerly drag the barrel to the ball.

This hitter is "feeling" for the pitch. Both his lead and front arm are still flexed after contact, which illustrates a conservative swing attempting to place the bat on the ball. His front leg is still bent (front foot hitting) and although this is an inside strike, his hips have only slightly rotated.

No Place for Passive Swings

There are several signs that indicate you're guilty of this fault. The most obvious is when you swing and miss a pitch. Instead of hearing or feeling that violent "whoosh" from your swing, you'll feel a more conservative swing. In addition, balls you hit off the sweet spot of the bat will travel a shorter distance. Infielders will gobble up ground balls in the hole because your hits lack sufficient speed to get through the infield.

Last, you'll be late on pitches, either fouling them off or swinging through them. Because you're tentative, your sense of timing is disrupted. Your adjustment will then be to start your swing earlier, which in turn gives you less time to recognize pitch type and location.

To hit the ball with authority, you've got to swing the bat with authority. Take short, violent cuts at the ball. Look to punish the incoming pitch. To be dangerous, you have to think dangerous.

> "Always anticipate the pitch is going to be a strike and that you're going to swing unless you see it's not a good pitch to swing at. When I've gotten into trouble, it's often because I'm not aggressive enough. I take too many pitches."
>
> — *John Olerud*

DRILL 1

■ With a coach or teammate feeding you soft toss from straight ahead, take strong, aggressive swings. Attack each pitch with ferocity. After each swing, check your balance to make sure you're not overswinging. Keep proper

With the pitcher behind a screen approximately 30 feet away, take strong swings and attempt to hit the ball through the screen.

mechanics in mind, but turn up the volume a bit and unleash a punishing swing. Maintain balance and cut it loose!

DRILL 2

■ Have a coach or teammate throw you short tosses from about 30 feet. The focus of this drill is to allow each pitch to travel as deep as possible before taking your cut. As the ball travels deep into the hitting zone, explode on the ball with a short, striking swing and speedy hip torque. You'll have to hit the ball a bit earlier on inside strikes, and a bit later on outside strikes. The object is to let the ball get as close as possible.

Fault #40 Overswinging

When hitters start thinking logically, it often becomes the bane of their existence. Surely at some time you've thought, "If I swing harder, the ball will go farther." You may never have said those words, but have undoubtedly swung the bat with that idea in mind.

Part of what makes Albert Belle such a dangerous hitter is his aggressive nature. On this swing, however, he's guilty of overswinging. By swinging too hard, he's pulled his head and shoulders off the ball and away from home plate. He literally "came out of his pockets."

If you meet the ball squarely with proper timing it will reach the bleachers. But only if you let it happen.

Stay Under Control

Overswinging is easily recognized. It's a swing without balance, timing, and grace. In fact, the batter looks more like he's flailing at the ball rather than swinging. If you find yourself losing balance in the follow-through, you're probably overswinging. If you're a millisecond late on a pitch "right down Broadway," you're probably overswinging. You're what hitting instructors describe as "too long to the ball."

Remember, a good swing is short in back and long in the front. Long in the back just gets you into trouble. When you swing too hard (or you "jack up" and become too long in the back) you create tension and tension is the enemy of the hitter. If you aren't relaxed and loose, your hands will have trouble bringing the barrel of the bat to the ball in time. You'll get jammed. On top of that, trying to swing harder means you'll be jerking your head and shoulders rather than using your normal smooth swing. This too will pull your head off the pitch. Remember to think, "Be quick to the ball and strong through it."

> "When I was younger, I would somtimes try to swing the bat too hard. But it's not productive. The harder you swing, the more prone you are to make mistakes. You want a strong swing, but you want it compact, in balance, and short. Long swings slow your bat down."
>
> — *Doug Glanville*

"When you try to hit the ball for power, sometimes your swing gets a little too long. When that happens, you might be late with your swing and get jammed, or pull off the ball too soon. The best thing to do is to stay back, see the ball, and then explode through it."

— *Dante Bichette*

Here is what baseball immortals Mickey Mantle, Ty Cobb, and Tris Speaker, all Hall of Fame members, had to say about overswinging. Read and heed.

Mickey Mantle: "Don't try to kill the ball. All well-hit balls, especially the long ones, come from balanced, well-timed swings. It's the same with the swing of a champion golfer. The theory is absolutely the same. The good ones don't press."

Ty Cobb: "Don't overswing for a long hit. This weakness causes slumps. After hitting a long and hard ball, the thought will come to mind that you did not swing hard. Actually, it was timing. And the next time up, you will be tempted to take an unnatural cut, trying for a still longer ball. Watch that, for as a rule the results are not good."

Tris Speaker: "I found that most slumps come from overswinging and over-striding. If you swing too hard you upset your sense of timing, and if your stride is too long you are able to apply but little of your power. So when you find yourself in a slump, shorten your stride and cut down also on your swing."

Left: Overswinging creates tension, slows your bat, and disrupts timing. The barrel drops and trails behind the hands from exerting too much effort. *Right:* Overswinging also causes you to lose balance. Hitters often begin to fall backward off-balance and use their bat to stay afloat.

A controlled swing allows you to maintain balance and keep your energy going to the ball instead of pulling away from it.

Fault #41 Rolling the Top Hand Too Soon

Many hitters are labeled "top-hand hitters." This means that their top hand dominates their swing and begins to roll over before contact. Instead of the hands remaining synchonized through contact, the top hand takes over the swing prematurely. This causes a variety of problems and limits your potential as a hitter.

Trying to Pull Promotes Top-Hand Hitting

There are several explanations for why you roll your top hand over too soon. The primary one is wanting to pull everything. Pulling the ball requires the barrel to be ahead of the hands as it contacts the outside of the ball. For this to occur, the top hand must take control of the bat handle and roll the wrist early.

Hitting the ball too far out in front of the plate promotes a top-hand dom-

Observe how quickly Scott Rolen's barrel moves up and out of the hitting zone. This is because he rolled his top hand too quickly, which raises the barrel. The result is a chopper to the infield.

inant swing. You're not letting the ball get to you. If you reach for the ball, the top hand automatically rolls its wrist to extend the bat outward. The correct contact area is a few inches in front of home plate (inside strike), just off the top edge of home plate (middle strike), or over the top portion of home plate (outside strike).

Timing is also a factor in a top-hand dominant swing. When you're fooled by an off-speed pitch, your hands (and the barrel) arrive too soon. Your brain has already told your hands when to fire the barrel. When the ball arrives late, your top hand has already started to roll over into your follow-through.

Check Your Starting Point

Many top-hand hitters hold their hands out away from their body in their stance and pre-swing movement. This induces you to "surround the ball" with your bat and hit the outside of the ball. Instead, try holding your hands closer to your body, approximately 6 inches off your rear shoulder. Keep your hands inside the ball as it approaches and then fire the barrel to the ball. *Remember, short to it and long through it.*

Loss of Power, Speed, Carry, and Control

As mentioned, several problems result from rolling the top hand too soon. The most critical is a loss of power and bat speed. Other troubles include poor bat control, no carry on balls hit in the air, and inconsistent contact. Here is why you lose power and bat speed.

It's no secret that two hands driving through the ball is stronger and quicker than one hand. Your lead arm is pulling the barrel and your top hand is pushing the barrel to the ball. Although these are two separate actions, the hands are synchronized as they take the barrel to the ball. If the top hand begins to roll over before contact, it has taken control of your swing and your bottom hand is now simply holding on to the bat. Try swinging the bat with one hand and you'll see and feel the dramatic drop off in speed and power.

Wrist Rolls—Barrel Raises

When the top hand begins to roll over, something else happens to your swing—the barrel raises. Grab a bat and slowly go through your swing. As you roll your wrists, pay special attention to the barrel. Notice the barrel raises slightly. If this occurs during your follow-through, it's insignificant. But if it's occurring as you make contact, it's problematic. Here's what happens when the barrel raises before or at contact.

1. Your barrel is traveling on a path to meet the top of the ball. Result: You'll either miss the pitch or hit a foul tip to the catcher.
2. Your barrel is traveling on a path to meet the middle of the ball. Result: You'll top a ground ball to the infield.
3. Your barrel is traveling on a path to meet the bottom of the ball. Result: You'll hit a top-spin line drive that dives or hooks toward the ground.

Ever hit a long fly ball that lost steam and dove out of the sky into the out-fielder's glove, or hit a line drive down the third base line that hooked foul? This happens because your top hand is active too early in your swing. The barrel raises up at the ball as it contacts it and puts top-spin on the ball, much like a tennis player does with his forehand. Stay through the ball with both hands and that long fly ball becomes a home run.

Big Mac's Record-Breaking Swing

If you witnessed Mark McGwire's record-breaking 62nd home run in 1998, you saw a perfect example of a hitter rolling his wrist too soon. His 334-foot, screaming line drive was a short poke compared to the 420-foot drives he

> "We make adjustments all the time. I don't think we do anything radical, but I think if you're smart you have to make some slight adjustments, whether it be mental or physical. If a pitcher is getting you out a certain way, or you feel something is a little off in your swing, you've got to do something or you'll continue to get beat."
>
> — *Scott Rolen*

A Time to Roll Over

A top-hand-dominant swing is not an ideal swing. But for left-handed hitters, certain game situations may call for you to alter your swing and roll the top hand over early. Consider this situation.

In the top of the first inning, your leadoff hitter doubles. As the next hitter to bat, it's your responsibility to get that runner to third base. This puts him in position to score on a ground ball or fly ball, giving your team an early 1-0 lead. To advance the runner, you need to hit a ground ball to the right side of the infield. To do so, hit a strike out in front of the plate, rolling the top hand over at contact. This adjustment will result in a pulled ground ball to the right of second base.

Remember, this is a "situational" swing. Use it to get the job done for the team. It should not, however, become your natural stroke.

averaged during that season. Why was his 62nd nearly 100 feet less than his average? Did he let up on his swing? Did he swing at a ball out of the strike zone? No. The answer is that he got a low, inside strike, opened his hips, and rolled his top hand over as he made contact with the pitch.

Fortunately for McGwire, he's an absolute monster. Despite the fact that he didn't stay through the ball with two hands, he's still strong enough to hit the ball over the fence. However, if you (or most humans) hit the ball using that form, the left fielder would have had to run in to make the catch.

McGwire made history with that swing (and 61 others), but it's not the swing that has made him one of the greatest home run hitters of all time.

Fixing Your Specific Problem

There are several causes for rolling the top hand too soon (trying to pull the ball, hitting the ball too far out front, top-hand dominant swing), and there are several remedies.

Trying to pull every pitch you see is a bad approach to hitting. You must abandon that mentality. There is a big field out there, and the best hitters use all of hit. A hit counts the same whether you pull a ball through the hole, or line one to the opposite field. Use batting practice to work on hitting the ball to all fields. One way to train yourself during batting practice is not to allow yourself to hit anything to the pull-side of second base. As stated earlier, keep your hands inside the ball as they travel to it, then fire the barrel. Another swing thought is to try to hit the middle-inside of the ball.

Let the Ball Travel

Hitting the ball too far out in front of the plate is very common. To eliminate this mistake, you must develop patience. Let the ball get to you. Work off the tee and get a feel for what it's like to hit the ball closer to the plate. You'll quickly feel how much more force your swing has, and you'll find it much easier to stay through the ball with two hands.

Isolate the Bottom Hand

To cure a top-hand dominant swing, you need to get a feel for the bottom hand's purpose. Understand that the bottom hand (and lead arm) aren't simply along for the ride. They add strength, speed, and guidance to your swing. To accomplish this feel, isolate the bottom hand in soft-toss drills. Choke up and hold the bat above the grip (about one-third of the way up the bat) with your bottom hand. During soft toss, hit balls straight back through the middle. Fire the barrel at the ball using your wrist and forearm (not your shoulder). This will be a difficult drill at first, but you'll quickly improve. After a dozen successful swings, add the top hand. Maintain focus on firing the barrel with your bottom hand.

DRILLS

■ Here are some drills specifically designed to accomplish hitting through the ball with both hands.

1. Place a batting tee at one end of the cage. Set your stance to the tee as if you were hitting a pitch down the middle. With each swing, attempt to hit line drives into the back net of the cage. If you fail to do so, adjust your swing accordingly. For example, hitting a ball into the pull-side of the net means you're using too much top hand. Feel the bottom hand stay through the ball a bit longer on your next swing.

2. For this drill you'll need a batting cage and two white towels. Place one towel on the right-hand side of the cage, a few feet below the top of the net, approximately 10 feet from the back end of the cage. Place the second towel in the same position but on the left-hand side of the cage. These towels are positioned to give the hitter a visual image. The object is to hit every pitch between the two towels. With a coach or teammate throwing batting practice, hit each strike between the two towels. This will force you to stay through each pitch with two hands.

3. This is a variation of the soft-toss drill. Take your normal swing to the ball, but just after contact, stop your bat. Do not allow the wrists to roll over and follow through. This develops the habit of keeping the wrists locked through contact.

Top left: To feel the importance of the lead arm, take soft toss with just the bottom hand choked up 6 inches on the bat. *Top right:* Hitting off a tee, visualize hitting through two baseballs. This will keep both hands hitting through the baseball and eliminate premature rolling. *Bottom left:* When stopping your bat after contact in soft-toss drills, you're able to observe if your top hand has rolled over prematurely. When properly executed, the hands should be in the palm-up, palm-down position, as shown here. *Bottom right:* Even the big leaguers spend time perfecting their swings. Here, Mike "The Hit Man" Easler tosses balls to St. Louis Cardinal outfielder J. D. Drew.

The Top-Hand Release—What Lau Really Meant

Charley Lau was one of the great hitting instructors during the 1970s and 1980s. Lau was an instructor with the Baltimore Orioles, Oakland As, Kansas City Royals, and New York Yankees. He passed away in 1984.

Around ball yards and batting cages today, Lau's name is synonymous with the top-hand release. But those who refer to him as a zealot of the top-hand release are incorrect. The truth is that Lau was an advocate of full extension, but not necessarily achieved by way of the top-hand release. Releasing the top hand, he felt, was one method by which hitters could achieve full extension, but if they reached full extension keeping two hands on the bat, he'd prefer they use that technique. Here's what Lau said in his book, *The Art of Hitting .300.*

"Now I'd be the first person to recommend keeping both hands on the bat—if you can do it and still get extended. A lot of major league players are able to do this, and their success is proof that the top-hand rule can work. But there are a lot who can't, and their top hands cause them a lot of trouble.

"I don't think it's correct to say that the top hand has to come off each time you swing. But at the same time I don't think it's wise to blindly follow the top-hand rule without giving any thought to your arm extension. This is why it can often be a good idea to work on taking the top hand off in practice, even if you keep both hands on the bat during the game. This way you'll be thinking 'extension' and be more inclined to get your arms out than someone who hasn't practiced taking his top hand off."

The top-hand rule to which Lau refers is the idea that at the point of contact, the top hand should roll over. Instead, Lau feels that the top hand fires the barrel to, and then through, the ball. The difference in outcome is "driving" the ball, instead of just "hitting" the ball. Driving the ball allows you to hit the ball harder and farther.

Releasing Too Soon

The problem many young hitters run into is that they release their top hand too soon. On most pitches, extension occurs just after contact, and if you're letting go with the top hand as you hit the ball, you're sacrificing both power and bat speed.

To observe someone who releases the top hand correctly, watch St. Louis slugger Mark McGwire. He releases his top hand but not until well after contact is made. Check out his swing in slow motion or in photographs. Both hands are still on the bat *after* he's hit the ball.

McGwire releases the top hand for the exact reasons that Lau taught—to achieve full extension of the arms. In the past, McGwire had trouble achieving full extension and often cut his swing short by rolling his top hand too soon. When he began releasing his top hand toward the end of his follow-through, he forced his hands to stay palm up, palm down through the ball. McGwire's results have been spectacular.

Keep in mind what Lau says, however. Experiment with the top-hand release only if you're failing to achieve full extension. Try it in practice and see if the results are satisfying.

When he is patient, Andruw Jones is one of the most dangerous hitters in the major leagues. Jones uses a slight inward knee turn as his coiling action *(this page, top left)*. He takes a soft, short stride to the ball. You can tell his stride is square because his hips are still closed *(this page, top right)*. Notice also that his front foot is planted before his hands move forward to the ball. His hands start down and are kept in close toward his

mid-section. His front leg braces *(this page, top right)*, allowing his hips to rotate and hands to fire forward. Jones keeps his bat on a level plane through the hitting area and eyes looking down at the point of contact *(previous page, bottom left)*. Although he releases his top hand during his follow-through *(this page, bottom right)*, it doesn't occur until well after contact has been made.

Ron Gant
Doug Glanville

The Mental Approach

Physical faults are fairly simple to detect. Detecting *mental* mistakes is a different story. It's tough to read a hitter's mind.

Effective hitters take advantage of pitchers through observation and calculated risks. They accomplish this by gathering information during the game and processing it through their hitting approach. The brain, however, can get a hitter into trouble if the *wrong* thoughts are lurking inside his head.

There are many different types of mental mistakes hitters make. Failing to know the game situation, fear of being hit by the baseball, fear of failure, and the very worst, lack of confidence, are just a few of them. Psychological faults not only contribute to slumps, they can ignite slumps.

Through time, you've probably been told not to "think" at the plate. There is certainly merit to that, but it's not quite so black and white. A clear and sound mind does allows you to focus on your intent. Too many nervous and erratic thoughts breed self-doubt. If you're saying to yourself, "I need to get my stride foot down and make sure my hands get back. . . . I've got to get my hips through with minimal linear movement," well, then, you're in serious trouble. You're overthinking, and the ball will be in the catcher's mitt before you can get the bat off your shoulder.

A single swing thought is okay, but it should be philosophical more than mechanical. Remember the movie *Bull Durham*, when catcher Crash Davis is at bat and repeats over and over to himself, "Quick bat, quick bat, quick bat, quick bat." This type of thought will not hinder your swing. Some other swing thoughts generate positive results, such as "hit the ball back through the middle," "drive through the ball," or "let the ball get deep." These thoughts inspire good swings without being mechanical.

Using Information to Your Advantage

There is information that materializes throughout a game from which you gain an advantage. This includes watching a pitcher's windup and timing his

> "Even though you may feel that you've maximized your ability as a player, there are still a lot of areas you can work on to improve performance that are not ability-related. Controlling your emotions is not ability related, being able to concentrate is not ability-related, being able to relax is not ability-related, being patient is not ability-related, enjoying being at home plate in pressure situations is not ability-related. None of those things have to do with your physical abilities, they have to do with what's going on inside your head."
>
> — *Hal McRae*

delivery, knowing what pitches he throws for strikes and what pitches he's having trouble controlling, recognizing where his release point is, if he alters it when throwing different pitches, and if he has any distinct pitch patterns. Being attentive and applying this data to your at bats can make life a little easier.

At times this information will be of great assistance and things will be clicking. Every thought and instinct you have is on the money. Ride that out as long as you can. There will be other times when everything seems to work against you; when every approach you take seems to be wrong and you sense that you're overthinking. This is when you should adjust and take the "see the ball and hit it" approach.

Relaxed, Quiet Confidence

This section will discuss how careless and negative thinking can adversely affect your performance at the plate. But before diving into that, there are two characteristics that are most important to a hitter's mindset: to be relaxed and confident. If you can always carry those two elements with you to the plate, you'll improve as a hitter.

A relaxed mind and body keeps the muscles loose and tension-free. This can be accomplished by deep breathing and taking control of your emotions. Try to slow everything down. The ball out of the pitcher's hand will look a little bit bigger and seem to travel a little slower when you're relaxed.

Confidence may be the most important factor in hitting the baseball consistently. You've got to believe in yourself and step up to the plate with presence. There is no hoping, no wishing, and no trying; just going up there to do the job. This does not imply strutting up to the plate in a cocky manner. It means quiet confidence—*knowing* you're better than your opponent, but keeping it to yourself. When you've developed quiet confidence, you've gained access to one of the secrets of hitting.

Fault #42 Fearful of Being Struck by the Ball

Former Boston Red Sox player and Baseball Hall of Fame member Carl Yastrzemski once commented on the fear of getting hit by a pitch, "If you're afraid of being hit, you might as well not bother going up to the plate at all. You can't hit the ball if you're afraid it will hit you."

His comments are true. You will never be successful if you let fear control how you approach hitting. However, fear of getting hit is natural, and all

Chipper Jones turns his front shoulder in to avoid being struck by the pitch.

baseball players deal with it. Only a fool wouldn't realize the danger of getting hit with a 95-mph fastball.

Stepping in the Bucket

Many players who are afraid of being hit by pitches step away from the plate when a pitch is thrown—what's known as stepping in the bucket. Pitchers who see this will take advantage by throwing pitches that move from the middle to the outside of the plate—pitches that the batter cannot reach. Unfortunately, batters who step in the bucket out of fear become one-dimensional hitters—they can hit only fastballs on the inside of the plate. Even curveballs that break over the inside of the plate won't be hittable because the fearful batter will flinch when the pitch starts toward him before breaking over the plate.

> "You can't be afraid of the baseball. You've got to attack the baseball."
> — *Jay Bell*

But fear need not paralyze you or prevent you from becoming a productive hitter. Fear can be overcome. Players need to replace their fears with a healthy respect for what can happen if struck by a pitch, they need to learn how to deal with errant or brush-back pitches, and they need to focus on the knowledge that getting hit by a pitched ball is not a frequent occurrence and that it rarely results in serious injury.

Guess Hitting vs. Reacting

Guess hitting can result in some big hits, but if you rely on it, those hits may come few and far between.

Guess hitting does have merit if it's an educated guess early or when you're ahead in the count. Many pitchers like to get ahead with a fastball and will groove a strike on the first pitch. In that case, look for a fastball in a certain spot. If it's there, attack it. If it's a different type of pitch or in a different location, keep the bat on your shoulder.

Pitchers often start middle of the lineup hitters with off-speed pitches. It's not unusual for a three, four, five, or six hitter to see a curveball on the first pitch. If this happens regularly, sit back and look for a curveball.

Guessing Deep in the Count

Troubles arise when you're guess hitting deep in the count. You can't afford to guess wrong deep in the count, especially with two strikes. Just take a look at the percentages. Suppose a pitcher has three different pitches. You have only a 33 percent chance of being correct. It's tough enough to earn a base hit when you know what pitch is coming, but if you cut those chances by two-thirds, your batting average will begin to plummet.

Good hitters *react* to pitches late in the count. They shorten their swing and attempt to see the ball as long as possible before committing their hands to swing the bat. The best approach is to look for a fastball, and adjust to an off-speed pitch. If a hitter looks for the off-speed pitch and is thrown a fastball, he won't have enough time to react. He'll be frozen, and on his way back to the bench.

Guess hitting is okay when it's an *educated* guess. Early in the count or when you're ahead in the count (2-0, 3-1), go ahead and sit on a pitch. But don't try to guess every pitch. If you do, you'll be second-guessing yourself from the dugout.

Learn to Dodge the Bullets

The first step in diminishing the fear of getting hit is to learn how to defend yourself against getting hit. The way to avoid serious injury when a ball is bearing down on you is to tuck your head behind your front shoulder and roll your body away so that your back faces the pitcher. Most of the time the pitch will miss, but if does hit you it will be off the arm or back or rear end, rather than the face, ribs, wrist, or hands. Your helmet will protect you from serious injury if you are struck by the ball in the head or ear area.

Serious injury, such as when a bone is broken or bruised, more often results from getting hit in the wrist, hand, lower arm or elbow, those parts of the body that are exposed if you continue moving toward the pitcher or spin toward foul territory instead of home plate. If your tendency is to fly open when a pitch comes at you, try wearing a protective guard over these areas, especially on the arm that is closest to the pitcher. Mo Vaughn and several other major league players successfully use them for protection while batting. Turning toward foul territory to avoid a pitch, however, is very dangerous and will inevitably lead to a painful injury.

Use a tennis ball to practice turning in and away from the pitch. You'll be surprised at how easily you escape the path of the ball.

DRILL

■ Balls thrown toward you that are above the waist present the greatest chance for injury. This drill will help you to protect yourself from getting seriously hurt. Practice rolling away from pitches by having a buddy throw tennis balls alternately for strikes and toward your body from the shoulder to the waist. When you see the ball coming at you, quickly roll your lead shoulder inward, tuck your head down behind it, and spin toward home plate and away from fair territory. Do this drill ten to fifteen times, then repeat. You'll soon learn to react correctly to pitches thrown toward you.

Fault #43 Fear of Failure

Every batter, at some point, has thought, "Oh man, I'm 0-for-3 right now. Please let me get a hit. I don't want to go 0-for-4." In that single thought, you've committed a fault. Before a pitch is thrown, you've reduced your chance for success.

Hitting is not a perfect science. There are too many variables to ensure perfection. It's an act that requires continuous evaluation, adjustment, practice, and improvement. Because it's so demanding, you must be of sound mind. Focus on the present. Don't dwell on the previous at bat (or pitch). The most important at bat or pitch is your next one.

Think Success, Put Failure into Context

> "I know it's tough but you can't get yourself hung up on numbers. If you go up and hit the ball hard, that's all you can do. You've done your job. You can't control the results."
>
> — *Travis Lee*

When it comes to hitting a baseball, you can't afford fear of failure. With hitting success comes failure too. What can make hitting psychologically draining is how quickly your brain has to shift gears. *Every time* you step into the box, you should assume you're going to get a hit. When you make an out, you have to calmly put things in perspective. Getting a hit every time is impossible. The best hitters in baseball history make outs seven times out of ten.

Consider three elite hitters (and their contributions to offensive baseball): Ty Cobb, owner of the highest career batting average in history; Rogers Hornsby, owner of the highest single-season batting average in the modern baseball era; and Larry Walker, the 1999 National League batting champion.

Cobb finished his career with a .367 lifetime batting average, so he made

Mark McGwire is congratulated by his third base coach after launching one of three home runs during a game in Philadelphia. McGwire feeds off positive thought and sees himself hitting the ball before he even steps up to the plate.

an out 63 percent of his at bats. Hornsby batted .424 in 1924, so he made 57.6 outs every 100 times to the plate. Walker won his second National League batting crown in 1999, hitting at a .379 clip. He is one of the most consistent hitters in the game today. But he still made 272 outs in 438 at bats during the season.

These numbers prove that the very best fail more often than they succeed. Failure is something they've learned to deal with. You must learn to deal with it as well. Don't ever accept failure, but don't fear the inevitable. Use each of your at bats, especially the unsuccessful ones, to become a better hitter, a smarter hitter.

Expectations

Beware of the expectations of others; they can place unnecessary pressure on you. Your job is to prepare yourself as best you can and give the maximum effort. Don't become fixated on your reputation, or what your parents and friends think you should accomplish. Understand your role and what your teammates need from you. Pressures from outside sources can distort your focus on what's important.

This doesn't mean you shouldn't set goals. Goals can help motivate you, as long as you set the right ones. Don't base your objectives on statistics. Do not enter a game thinking, "I've got to go 2-for-3 today to raise my average above .300." Instead, set general goals for yourself. "Stay off pitches out of the strike zone, and hit the ball hard every time up." If you stick to those types of goals, your batting average will take care of itself.

Visualization and Positive Thought

A poor mind-set can adversely affect your swing as easily as a mechanical fault. Anxiety and frustration create tension. Sweaty palms, an uneasy stomach, a tight grip on the bat, and impatience are all symptoms of tension. These symptoms will disrupt your rhythm, timing, strength, and quickness.

To avoid this, use visualization techniques to relax and foster positive thought. You may visualize something directly linked to hitting, or totally unrelated. Some people visualize hitting a pitch hard, or think back to a previous at bat where they experienced success. Others like to distance themselves from the field, and imagine being in a serene setting such as on a beach or near a river.

Find a method that works for you. Whether you imagine hitting the game-winning home run, or like to sing a tune to yourself, do whatever it takes. A clear, relaxed mind will make a major difference in your performance on the field.

DRILL

■ Timing and hitting a pitch perfectly doesn't guarantee a base hit. There are nine defensive players positioned to keep you off base. Conversely, you can make a host of mistakes and still manage to drop in a bloop double.

Write down all of the hard-hit balls off your bat that were caught during the season. Next, jot down all of the bloopers and "seeing-eyed grounders" that squeaked through for hits. (Be honest.) In most seasons, you'll find the two balance each other out.

This exercise indicates a fine line between what's considered a failure and what's considered a success when it comes to hitting a baseball. Getting upset between at bats is misspent time.

Fault #44 Lack of Confidence

Ever hear the cliché "Think bad thoughts and bad things will happen"? This philosophy speaks volumes when it comes to the art of hitting a baseball. Good hitters are confident hitters. If you lack confidence at the plate, it might be best to stay in the dugout until you find it.

A Tough Sport for Stats

> "You have to recognize that baseball is game where no matter how good you are, you're going to go through bad spells. You just have to stick it out, and work hard until you get hot again. It will happen. You have to be patient and believe in yourself and ability that things will turn around."
>
> — *Doug Glanville*

Confidence can be a tough sell to the psyche of a hitter; especially if the focus is restricted to results. Confidence is supported by success, and the success rate of hitters is lower than nearly every other trait in sports. Most would agree that the mark of a good hitter is .300. That means he bangs out a hit 30 percent of the time. Compare that same percentage to a quarterback (.530), a winning team's won-loss percentage (+.500), a ballplayer's fielding percentage (.950), or even a score on a math quiz, for that matter. It pales! Even the best hitters are humbled seven out of every ten times they go up to the plate.

Toss batting slumps into the mix. Every hitter, even the elite professional, goes through stages where he has trouble making solid contact. It's at this point that a hitter's confidence can really "take a hit." Unlike other team sports, you can't look to another hitter to bail you out at the plate. You're on your own, and it's up to you to get yourself back on track.

When a Slump Is Not a Slump

As many will agree, hitting slumps factor into fractured confidence. But it's important to understand what exactly is classified a slump and what should be more accurately labeled bad luck. Poor numbers do not necessarily consti-

Chipper Jones has such confidence that he dares pitchers to throw him a fastball.

tute a batting slump. Unfortunately, statistics in baseball are heavily scrutinized and viewed as indicators of success or lack thereof. It's not uncommon to hit four balls on the fat of the bat during a game, but the box score reads 0-for-4 the next day. Taking the collar does not mean you've fallen into a slump.

Do not create a slump psychologically. If you're hitting the ball well but have little to show for it, keep on plugging away. Don't press. The game has a way of evening itself out. The next time you smoke a line drive right at the center fielder, think about the bloop single that dropped in a week ago.

Bad Thoughts Equate to Bad At-Bats

Confidence is as fundamental to a hitter as the bat he uses and hitting style he selects. You must approach every at bat with the idea that you're going to get the best of the pitcher. Doubting yourself and your abilities will lead to failure. Negative thoughts beget tension. Tension, as stated time and time again, is the enemy of a hitter.

Lacking confidence will also make you timid at the plate. Instead of jumping on a good pitch you see early in the count, you'll find yourself waiting around for something better. It may never come. Timidity also may cause you

"When there is tension present, we're not confident, we can't concentrate, and we don't see as well. Everything is distorted when there is tension. One way to eliminate tension is to have a plan. How am I going to succeed in this situation? I'm not thinking about failing so it's all positive energy. Secondly, control your breathing. When you get in a panic, you can't concentrate. The plan is the first thing you do, so we're not thinking about any negatives. Two, control your breathing, and three relax. But the plan should relax you. For me, my plan was, "Don't get fooled." When I said don't get fooled, I stayed back and saw the ball better. Everyone is different, but hat's a plan that worked for me."

— *Hal McRae*

When you're struggling at the plate, there's no better place to start rebuilding your confidence than in the batting cage. If it's time well spent for Mike Piazza, it should be for you as well.

to "feel" for pitches instead of taking aggressive swings. This promotes hitting off your front foot and produces moderate hip rotation.

Go up to the plate knowing that you're given three strikes to hit with. Do not panic at strike one. Just because a pitcher gets ahead in the count does not mean you have to swing at everything he throws up there. Keep your cool and trust yourself. Some hitters (professional and amateur) are at their best with two strikes on them. It forces them to shorten their swing and use the entire field.

> "Confidence is as important to hitting the baseball as the bat in your hands."
>
> — *Will Clark*

Building Confidence

Confidence is not something that arrives overnight. Confidence is developed through hard work, meticulous preparation, and a strong mind. It's true that you can't control what happens once the ball leaves the bat, but you can control whether or not you're walking to the plate with confidence.

Confidence emerges when you know you've prepared for your turn at the plate. This develops through taking swing after swing in practice, and on your own time. Take so many swings during drills and batting practice that your swing becomes automatic. This is called muscle memory. That means when your eyes see a specific pitch in a certain location, they send a message to your brain and your body responds without hesitation. There is no shortcut to developing muscle memory. It simply takes hours and hours of practice.

Preparation alone will help your confidence. But if you do not put the time in, you'll have that same feeling you did when you took the science test without studying—insecure and doubting yourself. Work hard now, and reap the benefits between the white lines.

Visualization

Visualization is another technique that helps confidence and puts you in a positive frame of mind. Think back to the 1998 season when Mark McGwire shattered the single-season home run record by belting 70. Several images of McGwire come to mind. One is of him standing in the on-deck circle with his eyes closed, bat sitting atop his shoulder. McGwire was using visualization techniques to relax himself and stay positive.

This is not an exercise amenable only to home run hitters. Anyone can use it to his advantage. Whether you're in the dugout or on deck, visualize a great swing you've experienced. Think about the time you hit a line drive back through the middle, or when you blasted a ball over the left-center field fence. Maybe it will help to think about the swings you took in the batting cage before the game. Remember what that swing felt like and feed off it for your at bats in the future.

Any Information Is Useful Information

Each at bat is a personal battle between you and the pitcher. He is the one holding the ball, so you need to use any information attainable to offset his advantage. Watch for his pitch patterns. Does he start out with fastballs in the strike zone to get ahead or attempt to fool you with something off-speed? Will he come back with a breaking ball after he throws one for a ball, or does he always resort to the fastball? Does he tip his pitches in any way? Will he pitch to the outside corner early in the count and then come inside with a fastball?

Pay attention to release points and speed of motion. Pitchers often change their arm slot when throwing an alternate pitch. For example: fastball is thrown straight over the top, curveball is thrown with a three-quarter delivery. Any time the pitcher drops his arm a bit, you know to expect a breaking pitch.

Pitchers also have a tendency to alter their motion when throwing an off-speed pitch. The lower body speeds up, but the arm slows down. Watch for minor discrepancies like this to get a clue to what pitch is coming.

Any piece of information can help, but more importantly, you'll feel like you've done your homework. Preparation builds confidence. Good hitters are confident hitters.

DRILL

■ Before going to sleep at night, think about the five best swings you've ever put on a ball. It may have been when you were playing Little League, or it may have been the game-winning hit in your state championship game. Think about those swings and how they felt. Roll over and go to sleep.

Fault #45 Poor Judgment of the Strike Zone

Former major league outfielder Lenny Dykstra's thoughts echo those of the most successful major league hitters—it is important to learn and know the strike zone. What is the strike zone? It is an imaginary area over home plate between the batter's knees and his armpits. Any pitch thrown in this area is a strike. Knowing the strike zone can make all the difference in whether you develop into a good hitter or a poor one.

What causes poor judgment of the strike zone? The following behaviors can be significant causes: (1) inability to track and predict the path of pitches, (2) movement of the body and/or head and eyes, and (3) poor positioning of the eyes (one-eye tracking).

Repetitious Training Will Develop Judgment

If you do not have any serious eyesight problems, then the inability to track and predict the path of the pitches can be overcome with repetition. You can file the fault of moving your body, head, or eyes in the folder marked, "You can't hit what you can't see." If you are moving, your eyes cannot focus, process, and send the necessary information to the brain. The third cause—tracking with one eye—is cured by repositioning the head. Turn it toward the pitcher so that both eyes are focused and tracking the pitches.

If you develop a good eye, that is, you are able to quickly and decisively judge a thrown ball as either a ball or a strike, pitchers will have to give you good pitches. Good pitches are easier to hit. They're within easier reach, and you maintain your balance and ability to rotate the hips and deliver the barrel of the bat. However, if you show the pitcher that you do not have a good

> "If you want to be a consistent hitter, you've got to know the strike zone. Swinging at strikes not only increases your chances to hit the ball well and reach first base, but it also makes the pitcher work harder."
>
> — *Lenny Dykstra*

Left: A dangerous hitter like Andruw Jones becomes an easy out when he fishes for pitches out of the strike zone. *Right:* Scott Rolen watches this pitch all the way in.

knowledge of the strike zone, and you habitually swing at pitches outside it, you won't see a strike anytime soon.

Knowing the strike zone, of course, is only the first step in becoming a successful hitter. You must apply that knowledge in every at bat with a disciplined approach. This includes watching each pitch from the release point all the way into the catcher's mitt. Keep following the ball. Compare your judgment with that of the umpire. This is important because in reality the strike zone varies from game to game because different umpires will call the strikes as they see them.

To Each His Own

Despite its clear definition, the strike zone remains open to interpretation. Some umpires have a low strike zone, and some have a high one. One umpire may call a strike on a pitch that barely skirts the perimeter of the plate, while another may squeeze the pitcher and not give him the corners. You need to become aware of the "strike zone of the day" so that your approach matches what is being called that day.

Start while you are on deck, in the dugout, or even in the field. You can learn what will be called a ball and what will be called a strike. When you're at bat, note any pitches you judged differently from what the umpire called. Store that information and use it for the rest of the game. When you see that pitch again—and if the umpire called it a strike earlier—be ready to swing. Chances are good that if you don't, the umpire will call it a strike again. These borderline strikes—the pitches that are called differently by different umpires—are hittable. They just might not be the ideal pitch for you to hit, but with a disciplined approach, you do not sit back and take them for strikes. You attack.

If you do not know the strike zone and discipline yourself to hit strikes—all types of strikes—you will not succeed. It's that simple. Pitchers will take advantage of you.

DRILL

■ Developing a good knowledge should begin in pre-season. Here is a good drill for this.

Stand up at the plate while a pitcher is working his pitches. Assume the

To sharpen your judgment of the strike zone, stand up at the plate and take pitches. Call out "ball" or "strike" and compare your opinion with the catcher's.

The Umpire Is the Almighty Judge

An astute knowledge of the strike zone is a significant factor in good hitting. But don't fall in love with the thought that you own a "perfect eye." Too many hitters concern themselves with their personal judgment of the strike zone and fail to adapt to the most important person's judgment of the strike zone—the umpire's.

Umpires differ in their interpretation of the strike zone. Some have low strike zones, while others have high strike zones. Some umpires have a tight strike zone and hesitate to call pitches on the corners, while others have a wide strike zone and call pitches strikes that are off the plate. The important thing is that you adjust your zone to the ump's.

Sitting in the dugout complaining after called strike three doesn't do yourself or your team any good. Get the bat off your shoulder and protect the plate. One absolute in hitting that will never change is that you have to swing the bat to hit the ball.

stance you would take if you were batting in a game and treat the incoming pitch as if it were real. Pick up the ball when it leaves the pitcher's hand and try to determine how the ball is spinning, and its velocity and location. Step into the pitch and watch it all the way into the catcher's glove. Do not swing.

When the catcher receives the ball, have him call out whether it was a strike or ball and give the location of the pitch, such as "ball, low and outside." Note whether you agreed with the catcher's call.

After a few days of practicing this, add the next step. You call the pitches. While you are calling these pitches, have someone (a coach or teammate who has good strike-zone judgment) stand in the umpire's spot. Have him record his opinion and your call on a piece of paper. After ten pitches, go over the results. See if there's a particular location that you have difficulty judging regularly.

Repeat this drill daily, increasing the number of pitches from ten to twenty-five. Be sure to mix in a variety of pitches—sliders, curveballs, and change-ups. Your goal is to get 100 percent correct, nothing less.

Fault #46 Poor Judgment of Your Hitting Zone

In the movie *The Natural*, many will remember Pop Fisher, manager of the New York Giants, calling on unknown hitter Roy Hobbs to pinch hit. Despite being in his mid-thirties, Hobbs had yet to experience his first major league at bat. As he strode to the plate, Fisher yelled, "Come on, Hobbs, knock the

"What looks like a good pitch to hit to some may not look like a good pitch to others. It all depends on your personal preference and what lies in your hitting zone."

— *John Olerud*

cover off the ball." Quite a tall order, even for the most renowned professional hitter. But Hobbs, the ever-obedient cadet, hit the second pitch so hard that he literally knocked the yarn right out of its horsehide shell.

Cinematography aside, Hobbs had one thing in mind if he was to succeed in carrying out his manager's orders. In order to hit a ball *that* hard, it would have to be thrown in the perfect spot. Hobbs was not looking for a pitch in the strike zone, he was looking for something in his "hitting zone." Good hitters approach their at bats looking for something in their "hitting zone," not simply the strike zone. With fewer than two strikes, the hitting zone takes precedent over the strike zone.

Attacking the Pitcher's Pitch

Hitters who slump tend to wrongly focus on their mechanics. Often, however, it's their approach that needs tweaking. If your swing feels good, ask yourself these questions before tinkering with your mechanics. Does it seem like the pitcher always throws away from your strengths? Are you consistently making contact, but hitting balls weakly? Does it seem like your at bats are over quickly and you're hitting tough pitches? Are you rarely reaching first base via the base on balls?

The problem may not be with your stance, your stride, or your swing. You may simply be swinging at pitches in the strike zone but not in your hitting zone.

> "A lot of times you don't want to swing at an outside strike. You may want to wait and hope to get a mistake pitch that's easier to handle. The ideal place to hit a baseball is when it's over the middle of the plate."
>
> — *Jay Bell*

Hitting Zone vs. the Strike Zone

What, you might ask, is the difference between the hitting zone and the strike zone? Well, the answer is up to you. It's a matter of personal preference. The hitting zone is the area of pitch locations where you make the most consistent, solid contact. It's where you consider the pitch in "your spot." Ever have your father or coach throw you batting practice and ask you where you like it? You'll immediately put your hand out and say, "Right here." That is the central area of your hitting zone. The strike zone is said to be approximately seven balls wide by seven balls high. Your hitting zone might cover roughly half that area.

To define your hitting zone, pay attention to results during batting practice and games. Like almost all hitters, you crush pitches in certain locations and struggle with others. Collectively, the former locations make up your hitting zone. The latter spots are outside of your hitting zone. Once you become familiar with the hitting zone, you can use the information to improve game performance.

Too often, coaches tell hitters "get a strike to hit," or "look for a strike."

Although this pitch may be called a strike by some umpires, it lies outside of most batters' hitting zones.

That is too general. Look for a pitch specifically in your hitting zone. Here is a rule of thumb to live by: *Never swing at a pitch that is outside the hitting zone early or ahead in the count.* Swinging at a pitch outside your hitting zone early or ahead in the count is not the sign of a smart hitter. It shows poor patience. Do not make a pitcher's job easy by offering at a pitch outside the hitting zone. Even if the pitcher is purposely throwing to a spot that is outside your hitting area, remain patient and wait for a mistake. The rule book gives you three strikes. Don't be afraid to use them all.

Selective Hitting

As mentioned earlier, be selective early in the count and when you're ahead. Don't assume the word selective means simply looking for balls and strikes. It means getting a strike that you like. When ahead in the count (2-0, 3-1), shrink your hitting zone down to the size of two baseballs wide by two baseballs high. Don't swing at any pitch outside of that preferred area.

Even or down early in the count (0-1, 1-1, 2-1), be selective but to a lesser degree. Look for pitches in a zone that is approximately three baseballs wide by three baseballs high. In other words, you've slightly expanded the hitting

"My hitting zone was a little tighter than my strike zone. There are great bad-ball hitters in the game, Kirby Puckett was one of them, guys who swing at everything and still hit .300. I couldn't have success that way. I tried to hit only strikes."

—*Wade Boggs*

An aggressive hitter can be dangerous, but a patient hitter can be equally menacing.

zone to include more than the perfect pitch. This is known as being "selectively aggressive." A low and inside strike may be a pitch you want to attack if you handle it fairly well. If it's a strike down and away and outside your hitting zone, you should let it pass and look for something else. The object is to maintain an aggressive approach but not to go outside your hitting zone.

With two strikes in the count, you must now expand your hitting zone. You must "protect the plate." This may entail swinging at a tough pitch, but it sure beats being called out on strikes. By swinging, the batter at least has a chance of fouling the pitch off or putting it in play. Good hitters are able to spoil tough pitches (by fouling them off) and give the pitcher another chance to make a mistake.

> "Nearly every hitter has a certain type of pitch in a particular spot in his strike zone which he finds hard to hit. For some it's high and inside while others have trouble hitting anything that's low and away. On this kind of ball, and if the count is less than two strikes, take the pitch."
> —*Ted Williams*

Expanding Your Hitting Zone

The larger your hitting zone is, the more dangerous you'll become. Work to expand your hitting zone. To do this, you must recognize your weaknesses and work on turning them into strengths. If the pitch on the outside corner gives you trouble, spend part of every batting practice working on that pitch. Before long, you'll eliminate that weakness and broaden your hitting zone.

The easiest way to increase your hitting zone is to shorten your swing. This will eliminate "holes" in your swing. A short, compact swing provides the best chance of putting the barrel on the ball. You'll allow yourself to see the ball longer before committing your swing, handle pitches at higher velocities, and improve bat control.

Also, look for any glaring mechanical faults to eliminate weaknesses. A few examples: a hitch in your pre-swing movement can cause you to have trouble with pitches up in the strike zone; stepping in the bucket will make you susceptible to pitches on the outside part of the plate; holding your hands high may cause you problems handling low strikes. A simple adjustment in the pre-swing or stance may help you to expand your hitting zone.

DRILL 1

■ Take batting practice with the pitcher throwing from approximately 30 feet. Take five rounds of ten swings. During each round the pitcher will throw to a specific location. Each set should break down as such: first round—ten pitches down the middle; second round—ten pitches on the inside corner; third round—ten pitches on the outside corner; fourth round—high strikes; fifth round—low strikes. For each round, record your successes and failures. These results will give you a good indication of which locations lie within and outside your hitting zone.

DRILL 2

■ The only way to expand your hitting zone is to work on your weaknesses. Select three pitch locations (in the strike zone) that you have difficulty handling. Position the pitcher approximately 30 feet away and have him throw pitches to those specific locations. After three rounds (or thirty swings), move the pitcher back to 45 feet. After thirty more swings, have him throw the full distance (60 feet, 6 inches).

Fault #47 Failing to Recognize Pitch Patterns

The pitcher has a built-in edge in the batter-pitcher confrontation. He holds the ball, initiating the action at his leisure. You can only react to what he throws. That's why, as a hitter, it's important to gather every piece of available information. Recognizing pitch patterns offers you a means of some advantage of your own. Fail to, and you're hurting your chances for a productive at bat.

It takes approximately four-tenths of a second for the ball to get from the pitcher's hand to home plate. A hitter spends half that time swinging the bat. That leaves you with two-tenths of a second to pick up the ball out of the pitcher's hand, identify the type of pitch, and decide whether it's a ball or strike. If you have no idea of what pitch is coming, your chances of hitting the ball are reduced and the pitcher's chances of retiring you are increased.

Improving Your Success Rate Through Observation

Most pitchers (especially at amateur levels) fall into patterns when they're on the mound. They are predictable as to the types of pitches they throw, and the locations in which they throw them. Hitters who can detect a commonality in pitch sequences become very dangerous. Imagine that you knew the type and location of each pitch before it was thrown! Your batting average would soar!

Listed below are some examples of pitch patterns:

- Throwing a first-pitch fastball
- Throwing the breaking ball when the count is 0-1, 0-2, 1-2
- Throwing a fastball when he needs a strike (2-0, 3-1, 3-2)
- Throwing pitches out of the strike zone when ahead in the count

> "I know what the pitcher has before I go up to hit. It's in the back of my mind. When you work the count a little bit, you recall the information you've filed away. I'll remember what the pitcher has thrown me before in a particular situation. Depending on the count and game situation, I may look for a particular pitch, but for the most part, I'm just trying to get something out over the plate to drive."
>
> — *J. D. Drew*

Fearsome hitters like Gary Sheffield are fed a steady diet of breaking pitches. Here, his bat has already left the hitting zone before the pitch arrived.

Making Adjustments to the Pitcher—Facing Tom Glavine

Approach every at bat with your strengths in mind. Take the action to the pitcher; don't allow him to take the action to you. At times, however, you will have to give credit to a pitcher who's having success, when the approach that you and your teammates are taking is failing to produce results. In this situation, you must make an adjustment.

Tom Glavine is a perfect example of a pitcher who has consistent success with the same approach. He hammers away with fastballs and change-ups at the outside corner against right-handed hitters. From time to time, he'll come inside with a fastball to keep the hitter honest, then he'll return to the outside corner.

Glavine's stuff is a little above average by major league standards. He throws an 88-mph fastball, an excellent 80-mph change-up, and an occasional overhand breaking ball. He does not blow hitters away, nor does he rack up a huge number of strikeouts. But Glavine is very smart. He forces hitters to offer at pitches that are very difficult to hit with authority—pitches on the outside corner.

In this situation, you have to change your approach. You can't look for an inside fastball or a breaking ball over the middle of the plate because you may never get one. So you need to make an adjustment. Do something that will take him out of *his* game.

Former major league baseball player Dave Gallagher faced Glavine many times during his career. He tried several different approaches, and finally found that moving up on the plate and back in the box worked best when facing Glavine. This approach forced Glavine to think about busting Gallagher inside—a notion that was outside of his normal pitch plan, and one which allowed Gallagher to get better pitches to hit, namely, fastballs middle-of-the-plate and in.

"Guys would always say to beat Glavine, you have to take the ball to the opposite field. But do you know how hard it is to hit a ball hard on the outside corner—especially when he's changing speeds? Besides, Glavine is very smart and knows how to pitch. He reads everything you do as a hitter. When he sees you're diving across the plate and looking for the pitch away, he'll throw one in under your hands to keep you honest," Gallagher said.

"What I decided to do was to get up on the plate, and stand way back in the box. I moved up on the plate because pitching inside is what he liked to do the least. I thought if I forced him to do that, I was taking him away from his strength. Glavine pitches inside for effect, not to throw strikes. Also, now that I'm up on the plate, the outside corner pitch is like hitting a pitch down the middle. Anything that seems a few inches off the plate I now know is way outside.

"I moved back in the box so I could see the pitch a bit longer. Glavine paints the outside corner with his fastball, but he also has an outstanding change-up. So you're not only forced to swing at pitches in a difficult location, but it's also very difficult to detect and time his pitches.

"When I moved up on the plate and back in the box, I thought I finally had an edge on him. I could see the look on his face when he was out on the rubber that he wasn't happy with where I was standing. The last time I faced him I went 1-for-2 with a walk. I wouldn't say I owned him, but I think most hitters who've faced him would be happy with that."

- Following up an inside fastball with an off-speed pitch away
- Throwing pitches to the outside part of the plate
- Starting the next hitter off with a different pitch than the one that was just hit hard

Game Situations Dictate Patterns

Some pitchers have a set pattern that they rarely waiver from, while others adjust their patterns *during* the game depending on their success. It's your job to pay attention and think along with the pitcher. For example, if a pitcher notices his breaking pitch is getting hammered with regularity, he'll probably lose confidence in that pitch and won't throw it in a crucial situation. Another example would be a pitcher who throws a split-fingered fastball, but constantly throws it in the dirt. If you find yourself at the plate with a runner on third base, chances are the pitcher won't throw the split in fear of uncorking a wild pitch.

> "I never go up to the plate without a plan. The plan, however, depends on what you've seen from that pitcher, what his tendencies are, how you're feeling that day, what the game situation is, and what he's most likely to throw at that point in time."
>
> — *Will Clark*

Through process of elimination during an at bat, you should be able to make an educated guess as to what pitch is coming. When it's early or you're ahead in the count, you may want to put all your marbles in one basket. Look for a certain pitch in a specific location. If it's not the pitch you're looking for, let it go. Remember, you have three strikes.

With two strikes, you can't be as selective. Choke up a bit, shorten your swing, and just try to get the barrel on the ball. Do not try to "guess hit" with two strikes.

No facet of baseball is more enjoyable than hitting. There's no feeling like cracking a ball off the sweet spot of the bat. To achieve solid contact with regularity, you've got to pay attention to pitch patterns. On base, in the dugout,

Do not allow ballpark configuration to take you out of your game. The Green Monster at Fenway Park is notorious for tempting hitters to lift the ball to left field. Bat control artists can adjust with success, but most are victimized by producing flawed swings.

and in the on-deck circle, observe and absorb as much information as possible. It will help your confidence and the quality of your at bats.

DRILL

■ When watching a baseball game from the stands or on television, focus on what and where the pitcher is throwing. After you feel you've got a fix on his pitch selection and location, predict what he'll throw before each pitch. Take into account what pitches he has control of, how each hitter has performed, the score of the game, the inning, and the conditions of the weather and ballpark (dimensions, infield, etc.). If you can consistently guess along with pros such as Maddux and Glavine, you shouldn't have much trouble predicting the patterns of the pitchers you'll be facing.

Poor Situational Hitting

Situational hitting is an advanced form of hitting. When you reach the higher levels of baseball, you need to apply more than just basic hitting skills. You need awareness. Every time you go up to bat you need to know the score, what inning it is, how many outs there are, who, if anyone, is on base, what their capabilities are, who's on deck, and if there's any sign on.

Situational Hitting—Preparation Plus Awareness

Compile as much information as possible about the pitcher. What are his capabilities? Is he a strikeout pitcher? Finesse pitcher? Does he rely on sinking pitches that induce groundouts? Is he a high-strike pitcher? Is he likely to challenge you with his best stuff when he needs an out? Or will he try to trick you? What pitch does he go to in the clutch? If you haven't done your homework on the pitcher's tendencies and repertoire of pitches, you're dead meat! You're going into battle inadequately armed!

Situational hitting is being aware of what you need to do, of what you're expected to produce in each at bat. Many times you won't be over-thinking the situation—for example, with no one on base and two outs, you simply need to get yourself into scoring position. So first and foremost you'll be looking to drive a pitch into the power alleys for a two-base hit. However, with a runner in scoring position with fewer than two outs, the situation changes, and so does your approach.

Here are three situation faults that commonly plague hitters. Improve your game in these areas and you'll increase your value as an offensive player.

Fault #48 Failing to Move the Runner with a Sacrifice Bunt

Bunting is an important part of the game, and to be a complete hitter, you must learn to bunt. Becoming a good bunter will help your team and will increase your value as an offensive player.

Only Practice Makes Perfect

The most common fault among hitters is that they don't practice bunting enough. You may be under the impression that you're too good a hitter to worry about bunting, or that the bunt sign will never be flashed when you step up to the plate. The truth is, everyone is expected to bunt the ball. If you've failed to practice this craft and are called on to execute a sacrifice bunt in a crucial game situation, you're going to be up a creek without a paddle. And your coaches and teammates won't be happy.

Players make a variety of mistakes when attempting to bunt. Remember, this discussion is about *sacrifice* bunting. That means you are sacrificing yourself to advance a runner. In this situation, your primary goal is not to get to first base, but instead to get your teammate to the next base.

Note: There are two methods of sacrifice bunting: the square stance, where the hitter squares his feet to the pitcher; and the pivot stance, where the hitter simply pivots his feet and squares his upper body to the pitcher. Either method is acceptable and a matter of personal preference. Practice both and decide which brings the most comfort and success.

Failure to Achieve Full Plate Coverage

Chances are that you won't be able to take your normal position in the batter's box and achieve full plate coverage when sacrifice bunting. Unless your regular batting stance is very close to the plate, you will not be able to bunt the outside strike (upon squaring) without reaching for the ball.

To check your plate coverage, take your position in the batter's box and square around to bunt. From the bunting position, let go of the bat and allow it to drop to the ground. If the bat fails to cover the entire plate, you're standing too far from home plate. Move closer to the plate and forward in the box. This will also help you bunt breaking balls before they break.

"Won't this tip the pitcher and infielders that I'm bunting?" If the defense is observant, the answer is "yes." But remember, this is a sacrifice bunt. You're not trying to deceive the defense. The job is to advance the runner, not fool the infield.

No Flex in Your Stance

Don't stand tall (rigid) when squaring to bunt. It causes tension and makes the low strike difficult to handle. Flex at the knees to put yourself in comfortable, athletic position. Hold the barrel of the bat at the top of the strike zone. That way, everything above your barrel is a ball. Pull the bat back!

If the pitcher throws the ball low in the strike zone, use your legs to lower your body and put the bat on plane with the pitch. Do not drop the bat barrel down with your hands. You'll most often miss the pitch, pop it up in the air, or even worse, risk fouling it back off your face. Use your legs to lower your body, and keep the barrel above the ball.

Poor Bat Control

Move your hands up on the bat to improve your control. Do not leave both hands down on the handle. This reduces your control of the bat and allows the barrel to dip easily.

When sacrifice bunting, slide your bottom hand (left hand for right-handed hitters) up to the top of the handle (or grip). Slide your top hand just above the trademark. Holding the bat in these spots will give you excellent control of the bat, and because you're trying to bunt with the end of the bat to deaden the ball, this grip will keep your hands out of danger (from being hit by the ball).

Jabbing at the Ball

When a player bunts through the ball, nine times out of ten it's because he jabs at it. Keep your hands soft (tension free) and simply let the ball run into the bat. Don't poke at it.

Jabbing at the ball produces two types of bunting mishaps:

1. Missing the pitch
2. Bunting the ball too hard and allowing the defense enough time to throw out the lead runner

Extend the bat out as far as you can, and then relax your elbows. This puts the bat out in front of the plate, allows your eyes to watch the ball into your

> "The key to making good contact as a bunter is the exact opposite of what we teach for making good contact as a hitter. In hitting, the action we initiate thrusts the head of the bat toward the ball. In bunting, we want to let the ball come toward the bat. A big mistake bad bunters make is trying to jab the bat toward the ball. Once you've moved your bat into the bunting zone, the only time that bat, or any part of your body, should move is when the ball actually makes contact with the bat."
>
> — *Rod Carew*

bat, and keeps you from poking at the pitch. Simply keep the barrel at an upward angle, and "catch" the ball with the bat.

Holding the Bat Too Close to Your Body

Picture two riflemen on a firing range. One rifleman is holding his gun out in front of him at eye level, looking at the target. The other rifleman is holding the gun down by his side, tucked in toward his hip, looking at the target. Which marksman will record more accurate shots at the target?

The answer is the first rifleman because both his weapon and his target are within his sights. This generates better hand-to-eye coordination.

Bunting is no different. Do not hold the bat down and in toward your body. This makes it very difficult to bunt the ball consistently and accurately. Hold the bat out in front of you and bend at your knees and waist so you're holding the bat just a few inches below eye level. This way, you can see the ball longer, and look it all the way into your bat.

Dropping the Barrel Below the Ball

It's common to hold the bat perfectly parallel to the ground when squaring around to bunt (in a 9 o'clock to 3 o'clock position). This is a mistake. The natural tendency is to dip the barrel as the pitch is in flight. From this position, you'll most likely miss the pitch, foul it back, or pop it up.

Start with the barrel end of the bat angled slightly upward (8 o'clock to 2 o'clock position). This keeps the barrel above the ball or at least parallel to the ground after the bat dips a bit.

Squaring Too Late

It's unnecessary to let the entire world know you're bunting too far ahead of time, but you do need to give yourself ample time to get into bunting position. Squaring too late causes you to rush, which creates tension.

Preparation is a key factor in knowing when to square around. If the pitcher has a slow delivery (from the stretch position), start to square as soon as he lifts his stride leg. Quickly get your feet into position, extend the bat out in front of you, and bend your knees. Flex your elbows and look for a pitch below your hands.

You must square sooner if the pitcher has a quick delivery or uses a slide step. A slide step is when the pitcher does not lift his knee up in his delivery; he simply strides directly forward and delivers the pitch. In this case, it's best to begin squaring around when he comes to the set position (when his hands come to rest near his midsection). This tips the defense early, but it's better to be safe and make sure you get the bunt down.

Top left: The batter is dipping the barrel of the bat. This will induce the hitter to miss the pitch or pop it up. *Top center:* The barrel is held up, but the batter is not achieving full plate coverage. He must move closer to the plate to handle the outside strike. *Top right:* The bat is held in too close to the body. This diminishes your hand-to-eye coordination and ability to bunt the ball with soft hands. Get the bat out in front of you where you can see it. *Bottom left:* The batter keeps the barrel on top of the ball and bunts it safely to third base. *Bottom center:* This pitch is out of the strike zone, so the batter pulls the bat back in time. *Bottom right:* On low strikes, use your legs to lower your body to the pitch, rather than dropping your barrel to the ball.

Squaring Too Early

It's also possible to square too early. Again, a sacrifice bunt is not meant to be deceptive, but there's no reason to show the defense you're bunting earlier than you have to. If you're squaring around as the pitcher is taking the sign or before he comes to the set, you're squaring too early.

Two problems arise when squaring too early. The first is that it gives the defensive players (mainly the first and third basemen) too much time to charge the plate. If they're able to get within 20 feet of you before you bunt the ball, they'll be able to field the ball quickly enough to throw out the lead runner.

Second, standing for a long period of time in the bunting position can create tension. When hitting, you don't step into the box and get right into your stance. You move the bat a little and stay in motion as long as you can. If you square too soon, you'll be standing there like a statue, which will inevitably produce poor results.

Running Before the Ball Is Bunted

It can't be said enough times: Bunt the ball first, see it on the ground, and then run to first base. It is not a footrace for a base hit. It's a sacrifice! If you're concerned with getting to first base safely and try to rush, chances are you'll bunt the ball poorly. Remain stationary in the bunting position, bunt the ball on the ground, and run. It's as simple as that.

Where Should I Bunt the Ball?

Many coaches will tell you to simply get the ball down on the ground when sacrifice bunting. But the truth is, there are specific areas you should try to bunt the ball depending on the game situation.

First and foremost, do not bunt the ball back to the pitcher. He is the closest fielder, and his momentum is taking him toward home plate. A good fielding pitcher will either throw out the runner trying to advance, or worse yet, start a rally-killing double play.

With a runner on first base, bunt the ball to the first-base side. The first baseman is holding the runner on and will not be able to charge the ball as quickly as the third baseman. He also has his back to the advancing runner. Make the first baseman field the ball and the runner should have no problem advancing to second base safely.

With a runner on second base, make the third baseman field the ball. Here are two reasons why. If the third baseman fields the ball, it's very difficult for him to catch the ball, turn around, and fire an accurate throw to third base. Keep in mind that the runner on second base has a bigger lead than he does

> "You may be the best hitter on your team, hit in the three-hole, and never be asked the bunt. Once you move up to the next level, whether it be Babe Ruth to high school, or high school to college, you may be hitting eighth and asked to bunt with regularity. Bunting simply takes practice. It's a phase of your game that can be a strength or a weakness, which of the two simply depends on your efforts."
>
> — *Dave Gallagher, college and professional hitting instructor*

on first, and is also anticipating the bunt. He should get to third base in a very short period of time.

Second, by making the third baseman play the ball, the only way third base will be covered is if the defense is running a rotation play where the shortstop breaks early to cover third base. It's very difficult for the shortstop to sprint to third base, break down and get in position at the bag, catch a throw from the third baseman, and apply a tag—all before the runner arrives. Bunt the ball to third base, and the lead runner should have no trouble advancing.

DRILL 1

■ Make bunting a regular part of batting practice. Before taking any swings, bunt two balls to first base, two to third base, one drag bunt for a base hit, and one suicide squeeze. Do not allow yourself to swing the bat until you successfully complete the bunting exercises.

DRILL 2

■ To practice bunting accuracy, place a bat on the ground parallel to the third base line about 12 feet inside the foul line and 15 feet from home plate. Place a second bat parallel to the first base line, 12 feet inside the line and 15 feet from home plate. Alternating between first and third base, try to bunt the ball in between the bat and the foul line.

Fault #49 Failing to Score the Runner from Third with Fewer than Two Outs

With a runner on third and fewer than two outs, it's your job to score the runner. First, look at the infielders. There are three basic positions they can take: normal depth, "corners up" (the third and first basemen move up even with the bag), or on the grass. Your hitting approach changes according to how the infielders deploy.

If the infielders remain at normal depth, you can assume that they have decided to concede the run and will play to retire the batter (you). This situation is commonly encountered early in a game, when the opponents feel that

Part of Big Mac's success is linked to his patience at the plate. When a pitcher serves one up in his zone, however, he jumps into attack mode. Here, he launches one into the bleachers at Veterans Stadium.

"You've got the bases loaded with nobody out. What's my job as the hitter? What is my plan? Is it to hit a home run? No. Is it to get a single? No. My plan is to get a ball up in the strike zone, and hit a sac fly. That's my job. What happens is the hitter tries to do too much and tries to get all the runners in with one swing. Then he tenses up and is late with the barrel. When you simply think about getting a pitch up and hit a sac fly, you might hit a home run. You might drive them all in. The more we try to do, the less we accomplish. The less we try to do, the more we accomplish."

— *Hal McRae*

a single run will not decide the game and are confident that they can score runs to go ahead when they take their turns at bat. Opponents will also concede a run in almost any inning when they have a big lead and can afford to trade an out for a run. Knowing that your opponents prefer to retire you rather than prevent the run from scoring dictates your hitting approach. Aside from the obvious—a clean base hit—you have at least two ways to score the runner while making an out:

1. A fly ball, preferably deep, to the outfield
2. A ground ball to anyone in the infield except the pitcher

Be aware, however, that a strikeout pitcher may try to strike you out, thus stranding the runner at third. Here is an approach that may help you should you get into this situation and fall behind in the count. This approach assumes you are a right-handed batter trying to score a runner from third base.

Pitchers are taught to work away early in the count and to work inside late in the count. This pattern plays to the strength of a hard-throwing strikeout pitcher. With two strikes on a batter, a fastball that bores inside is a good pitch to throw. The pitcher is hoping that you swing and miss altogether or that you make weak contact, for example rolling a soft grounder back to the pitcher or third baseman. The runner will have difficulty scoring on either of these ground balls.

So with two strikes, choke up on the bat, widen your stance, and move slightly away from the plate, perhaps 2 to 3 inches—these adjustments will make sure you can get your arms extended and not get jammed, and they will give you better control of the barrel of the bat. Now, concentrate on hitting the ball where it's pitched. This will work strongly in your favor. Because you're slightly off the plate, any pitch thrown inside in an attempt to jam you will be a ball. Any pitch not thrown far enough inside will be met with the fat of the bat and driven to the center and opposite part of the field. If the pitcher tries to slip a pitch by you on the outside, he's playing into your hands. Simply reach out and slap a ground ball to the right side. Bingo! You've knocked in the runner from third.

Pitchers like to get ahead in the count in run-scoring situations. It allows them to work the edges of the plate later in the count. So in a situation with a runner on third and fewer than two outs you can often count on the first pitch being in the strike zone. It is often a good pitch to attack. A caution: don't hit a pitch that fools you, that is, upsets your timing, and don't hit a pitch that isn't located where you can drive the ball where it will score a runner. Last, don't be anxious in this situation. Remember, it's the pitcher who is in a jam, not you.

If the defense plays with the corners up (third and first basemen playing even with their respective bases), they will go for the play at the plate if the ball is hit to first or third. Otherwise, they'll go for the out. You should aim up the middle—a long fly ball or ground ball will do the job.

If your opponents aren't willing to give up a run (usually in a close game in the late innings), they will play on the grass. Rod Carew terms this scenario "the easiest way to hit .500." Simply try to hit the ball hard on the ground and slip it past the drawn-in infielders. With the defense playing in close, their range is so severely limited that only a ball hit directly at them is catchable.

You can also lift a fly ball into the outfield for a sacrifice fly. The surest way of accomplishing this is to hit pitches that are at least belt high in the strike zone. You are more likely to contact the ball below its equator and thus lift it into the air. Pitches below the belt can be lifted too but are also likely to be hit on the ground. The key is to hit the ball sharply—if you do, you might even smack a line drive for a clean RBI hit.

A batter's most flagrant offense (and poor situational hitting practice) is not recognizing that a productive out—a ball hit to a fielder who is conced-

"You've got to be patient enough to get a ball you can drive in the air. Take into consideration that the pitcher understands the situation, and knows what you're trying to do. He's going to try to combat that by trying to get you to chase. If you're patient, you can force him to give in and throw the pitch you're looking for."

— *Sonny Pittaro, college coach*

ing the runner scoring—will get the job done. Don't go brain dead when your teammates need you to score a runner. Poor situational hitting habits also include chasing pitches on the margins of the strike zone early in the count and swinging at pitches that are impossible to put in play in the direction and area of the field that you've determined will get the job done.

Fault #50 Failing to Advance the Runner from Second to Third with Nobody Out

With a runner on second base and nobody out, your job is to hit a ball to the right side of second base. The runner will advance to third base, then score on a fly ball to the outfield or ground ball to the infield (assuming they're not drawn in) by the next hitter. This is how you "manufacture" runs.

Hitting the ball to the right side of second base is a skill you must learn. The need to execute this occurs frequently in games, and it's important that your coach believe you can get the job done. Although you're sacrificing your at bat to move the runner, you're at least granted the opportunity to swing the bat. There's a chance you can hit the ball in the hole or drive the ball in a gap for a hit. If you can't execute, your coach will flash the bunt sign to make sure the runner advances.

Right-Handed Hitters

Hitting the ball to the right side of the infield is simple, yet right-handed batters often stuggle with this chore. The most common mistake you'll make is not allowing the ball to get deep enough in the hitting zone. Coaches preach to look for an outside strike, but the most important detail is to let the ball travel deep into the hitting zone. If you hit the ball out in front of the plate, you'll pull it whether it's inside or outside.

Quiet down your hip rotation. For this swing, your hips can't fully rotate. It will cause your barrel to jump out in front of home plate. As you make contact, your hips should face the second baseman, not the pitcher.

This is one situation where an inside-out swing (see page 119) is justified. It helps to direct the ball to the right side of second base. To do this, allow your bottom hand to lead your swing through the hitting zone. This will keep the barrel back and angle the bat to the opposite field. Don't let your top hand be too active in your swing. It will produce ground balls to the left side.

There's no question that it's easier to hit an outside strike to the right side of the infield. Take advantage of an outside strike when it's thrown to you. But focus on letting the ball get deep in the hitting zone. That's the key to hitting to the opposite field.

Left-Handed Hitters

If you're a hitter who loves to pull the ball, then this is your ideal situation. Make contact with the pitch out in front of home plate, and fire your top hand early in the swing. This will produce a ground ball to the right of second base. Full hip rotation will help you get the barrel out in front of home plate.

DRILL

■ With two or more teammates, take ten swings with the intent of hitting the ball to the right side of second base. After each swing, apply the proper point total to your result. A ground ball between the shortstop position and the second base bag is worth five points. A ground ball to the right side of second base is worth ten points. A line drive in the right-center field gap is worth ten points, and a deep fly ball to right field is worth five points. (The fly ball has to be deep enough that the imaginary runner could tag up and advance to third base.) The hitter who accumulates the most points wins the game.

Batting practice is the best time to improve bat control. Many major league hitters use their entire first round of swings to work on hitting the ball to the opposite field.

Glossary

athletic position   A "stance" that athletes use as a solid base or foundation from which to execute efficient physical movements. The feet are slightly farther than shoulder-width apart, knees flexed, and a slight bend at the waist. Think of a guard playing defense in basketball, a goalie in soccer, or a tennis player preparing to receive a serve.

barrel   The top part of the bat, where the diameter is greatest. You want to hit the ball with the barrel of the bat.

barring the lead arm   An action where the lead arm (or bottom-hand arm) is locked rigid when the bat is moved back to the launch position. This lengthens the swing and reduces bat speed.

bat speed   The velocity with which a hitter swings the bat. The greater the bat speed, the farther the ball will travel.

batting average   A statistic that measures a player's ability as a hitter. It is expressed in thousandths and is calculated by dividing the number of hits by the number of at-bats. In professional baseball, the standard of excellence is a batting average of .300, which means the player averaged 3 hits per every 10 at-bats.

casting   A movement where the hands are moved out and away from the hitters body as he begins his swing. The hands "cast out" and hit *around* the ball instead of taking a direct path *to* and *through* the ball.

choke up   To move one's hands up the handle of the bat away from the knob. Batters choke up to gain greater control of the bat.

coil   A pre-swing movement that moves part of the hitter's body away from the pitcher before striding forward and then swinging. A coil can be a slight inward turn of the front knee, a sway of the hips, or knee lift. This is also called "loading."

double-cock   A swing fault occurring when the hands move upward after reaching the launch position. This second movement causes the swing to be late to the ball.

drag bunt   A bunt purposely hit away from the pitcher in an attempt to get a hit. This is different from a sacrifice bunt where the batter's main goal is to advance a runner.

drifting   A movement in which the batter allows his weight to carry forward onto his front foot, which also moves his hands and head forward. This premature weight shift puts the hitter in a weak position to swing the bat, diminishing his hand speed and hip rotation. As a result, power and bat speed are lost. The accompanying head movement makes it difficult to track the ball and identify the type of pitch and its location.

follow-through   The continuation of the swing by the batter after the ball has been hit or missed. The follow-through is essential, because to gain maximum hitting power you must hit through the ball.

grip   The manner in which the batter holds the bat. Some batters grip the bat down near the end at the handle, others choke up. Ty Cobb, one of the greatest hitters of all time, gripped the bat with a space between his hands for greater control.

guess hitter   A batter who tries to anticipate which type of pitch is coming. Hitters who guess what pitch a pitcher is going to throw do so based upon the game situation (count, score, men on base, etc.). They also take into account their past experience against the pitcher and any pitching pattern they have observed during the game.

hitch   A pre-swing movement where the hands drop down toward the mid-section as the hitter strides. This additional movement can adversely affect the hitter's timing. Also, hitters who hitch have difficulty handling pitches up in the strike zone.

hitter's pitch   A pitch type and location that the batter generally hits with success. It's usually thrown when the pitcher is behind in the count (2-0, 3-1). A fastball down the middle is a hitter's pitch.

hitting zone   An area where the hitter likes his pitches. Most of these lie within the strike zone, but some can be outside of the strike zone. Furthermore, some areas of the strike zone are not a part of the batter's hitting zone. Each batter has his own hitting zone.

inside-out swing   A swing where the batter's hands are ahead of the bat barrel as the ball is contacted. The lead arm dominates the swing. Most inside-out swings result in the ball being hit to the opposite field.

launch position   The position the batter is in just before he swings the bat. His front foot is planted on the ground after the stride and the batter's hands are cocked just behind his rear shoulder. This is also known as the ready position.

leadoff hitter   The first player in the batting order. This position is usually occupied by a contact hitter who is also a fast runner. The first batter in an inning is also called a leadoff hitter.

overstriding   A stride that travels too far toward the pitcher. It inhibits hip rotation, which limits power and quickness.

overswinging   A swing fault in which the hitter swings the bat too hard. It creates tension in the hands and slows the bat down. Often, the head and front shoulder pull off the ball when overswinging. This results in swings and misses and fly balls to the opposite field.

palm-up, palm-down position   The position at contact where the top-hand palm faces up toward the sky and the bottom-hand palm faces down toward the ground. This is the proper position at contact. It shows the wrists have snapped the bat into the ball but have not yet rolled over.

pepper   A practice drill involving one batter and several fielders. The ball is pitched to the batter who hits the ball on the ground to the fielders. Whoever fields the ball throws it back to the batter and the sequence is repeated. Players use pepper as a way of loosening up for the game and as a means of improving hand-eye coordination and bat control.

pitcher's pitch   A pitch type and location that is difficult for even the best hitters to handle. It's usually thrown when the pitcher is ahead in the count (0-2, 1-2), and is often out of the strike zone. A breaking ball thrown low toward the outside corner is a pitcher's pitch.

plate coverage   The hitter's ability to contact pitches over the entire plate area. This includes pitches on the inside, middle, and outside portions of home plate.

ready position   *See* launch position.

release point   The point in his delivery at which the pitcher lets go of the ball. Smart hitters focus their eyes on the release point to get the best and longest possible look at an incoming pitch.

rolling the wrists too soon   A swing fault where the top hand rolls over prematurely so that its palm faces the pull-side at contact. This results in ground balls to the pull-side. At contact, the hands should be in the palm-up, palm-down position.

sacrifice bunt   A bunt where the batter bunts the ball with the sole purpose of advancing a runner. The hitter is not charged with a time at bat for a sacrifice.

sacrifice fly   A fly ball caught in the field of play that allows a base runner to score without an error being committed. The batter is credited with a run batted in (RBI) and is not charged with an at-bat.

separation   The act of the stride moving forward as the hands move backward. The upper and lower half of the body are moving in separate directions.

slump   When a batter has an extended period of poor hitting performance, he's experiencing a slump. Poor results should not be confused with poor performance.

spray hitter   A batter who hits the ball to all parts of the field but without much power.

squeeze bunt   A bunt that is executed as a runner from third base is advancing toward home. The play is often called a suicide squeeze because if the batter fails to execute the bunt properly the runner will be "dead" at home plate.

stance   The position assumed by the batter in the batter's box as he awaits the next pitch. Hitters vary their stance, but it's important to set up in a comfortable and workable position. When the batter's front foot is farther from home plate than his back foot, the stance is open; when the front foot is closer to home plate the stance is closed; when both feet are parallel to the closest edge of home plate the stance is square.

step in the bucket   When the batter's front foot moves away from home plate during the stride, he has stepped in the bucket. It is very difficult to hit the ball successfully if you step in the bucket. You will lose power and become vulnerable to outside strikes. Your front foot should go toward the pitcher during your stride.

stride   A batter's step toward the pitcher before swinging. Depending on the size of the hitter and length of his legs, the stride length varies from 4 to 8 inches. Most good hitters have short strides. A long stride is not recommended because it tends to lower the head (and eyes) too much.

strike zone   An imaginary area over home plate between the batter's knees and armpits. Any pitch thrown in this area will be called a strike if the batter doesn't swing. As any batter will tell you, each umpire has his own interpretation of the strike zone.

strikeout   When a batter swings and misses with two strikes or does not swing at a pitch in the strike zone with two strikes, a strikeout is recorded. A strikeout is also recorded if a batter attempts to bunt with two strikes and bunts the ball into foul ground.

sweet spot   The place located on the barrel of the bat that is most ideal for hitting the ball. A ball that hits the sweet spot receives maximum transfer of energy from the bat.

swing   When you move the bat in an attempt to hit a pitched ball, you have created a swing. It's also called a cut or a rip.

swing fault   A mechanical flaw or breakdown in the swing that causes or contributes to poor performance. The problem may exist in the batter's stance, pre-swing, or swing. A swing fault may also originate in the hitter's mental approach.

swing path   The route the bat travels after it leaves the launch position. The optimum course is one that travels directly to and through the ball. The bat should move forward and downward, then level off or travel slightly upward through the hitting area, and finally ascend into the follow-through.

timing   The ability of a hitter to gauge the speed and path of a pitched ball and then to swing his bat so that it collides with the ball at the proper point of contact.

trigger   A movement that initiates your swing. A hitter's trigger can be an inward shoulder turn, a toe tap, or even a hitch, such as with all-star Barry Bonds.

uppercutting   When a hitter swings the bat on an upward arc, he is uppercutting the ball. He will most likely hit fly balls and pull ground balls.

Index